Foreword

In general shipwrecks are disastrous even
and picturesque coastline, or in our wide estuar.
of our verdant rivers, then in the public's eye they acquire an air of romance.

These wrecks were reported in the papers of the times and are a mere fraction of all those lost at sea. This was highlighted in the 1860 *Journal of the National Lifeboat Institution* which stated that as the road system was primitive and the railways in their infancy, the majority of world-wide and British commerce was carried by sea. But the general public failed to realise that shipwrecks were a daily occurrence, affecting both the families, homes and counting-houses countrywide. The journal also highlighted the facts that as most shipwrecks occurred out of sight at sea, they frequently failed to raise any public emotion or to arrest any attention.

Today, rightly, great play is made of disasters a fraction of this magnitude, so it is incredible that formerly death and disaster on such a scale passed almost unnoticed. However, the old adage says it all '*Where he goes, and how he fares, no one knows, and no-one cares*'.

Even in the late thirties the great master of the monologue, Stanley Holloway recited:

There's a famous sea-side town called Blackpool,
that's noted for fresh air and fun,
and Mr and Mrs Ramsbottom went there with young Albert, their son.
A grand little lad was young Albert, all dressed in his best; quite a swell,
with a stick with an 'orse's 'ead 'andle,
the finest that Woolworths could sell.
***It wasn't very exciting**, the waves were fiddly and small,*
*there were **no wrecks, and nobody drownded,***
***in fact, nothing to laugh at, at all**.*

In Dartmouth over the centuries, local affairs and events including wreck and distress were mainly un-recorded until Robert Cranford in 1854 founded the *Dartmouth Chronicle*, often referred to as *The Chronicle.* This newspaper was meticulous in detail and recorded everything, including events of misfortune and those of a more tragic nature, particularly shipwrecks and nautical disasters, and it has been the principal source for this booklet

The long list of wrecks and other disasters in or around the Dart recorded in the following pages took place during a continuing expansion over the years of sea borne trade and in the growth of both Dartmouth and Kingswear. References have been included at appropriate points in the text to some aspects of special interest or significance and a full account can be found in the author's *The Chronicles of Dartmouth*.

Contents

ELIZABETHAN WRECKS

There are conflicting stories about the *Nuestra Senora del Rosario* and the *Madre de Dios* but the majority opinion suggests they both came to the River Dart and the remains of the *Madre de Dios* may still lie in Old Mill Creek.

1 1588 *NUESTRA SENORA del ROSARIO* an Armada flagship

She was the Capitana (flagship) of the Andalusian squadron captained by Don Pedro de Valdés, third in command of the Spanish Armada, and was the biggest ship in the Armada fleet. She had 51 guns, 117 crew and 300 soldiers as well as 30,000 escudos, a third of the money in ducats and gold earmarked for operations in England. In going to the aid of a badly damaged ship somewhere south of Dartmouth, *Rosario* collided with the *Santa Catalina* losing her foremast and bowsprit and becoming unmanageable. The leader of the expedition the Duke of Palma, on advice from Diego Florez who was King Philip of Spain's adviser, refused to risk the expedition by stopping the fleet to help the *Rosario*. It appears both the Duke and Diego Florez bore Don Pedro a grudge and the Spanish fleet pressed on leaving Valdés to fend for himself. Against orders, Sir Francis Drake in the *Revenge* left his comrades for the sake of a fat prize. Although the *Rosario* was larger and more powerfully armed and manned than the *Revenge*, rather than risk a fight with England's most celebrated seaman, Valdés accepted Drake's terms and surrendered. His crew's lives would be spared, but no mention was made whether they would be fed.

Drake then commissioned Sir Walter Raleigh in the *Roebuck* to tow the *Rosario* to Torbay where the officers received special treatment, while the crew were imprisoned in the Great Barn at Torre Abbey. Soon two hundred of the men were moved to Exeter gaol for eventual ransom and the *Rosario* and the remaining prisoners were moved to Dartmouth. William Henley, Dartmouth's self-taught mastermind, described their fate in correspondence in the *Chronicle.*

'At that time in warfare, it was not customary to take prisoners, as all the vanquished, wounded and well were tossed into the sea, in a practice called creating 'water spaniels'. Instead, those men held at Dartmouth died of disease brought on by starvation, as their provisions had gone bad and their bread was full of worms. Sir George Carey, Devon's Lord Lieutenant, said they should have been made 'water spaniels' when captured. Here we had a valuable prize containing Armada funds, powder, cannon, spices, swords, etc, but we showed no humanity. It is hard to believe our forefathers of so short time ago allowed such a tragedy to be enacted on the placid waters of our lake-like harbour. The bigotry of Philip (of Spain) and his inquisition was met here by bigotry as merciless as his own.'

In 1589 the *Rosario* sailed from Dartmouth to Chatham and then to Deptford. The surviving prisoners were finally freed on 24 November, 1590 and Valdés was ransomed shortly after. Whether the *Nuestra Senora del Rosario* ever sailed thereafter is unknown but it seems unlikely. In 1618, still in Deptford, she was cleaned '*of all the slubb (*sic*), ballast and other trash within board, making her swim and removing her near to the mast dock where she was laid and sunk for the defence and preservation of the wharf there.*'

2 1592 *MADRE de DIOS* a great carrack and treasure ship

In 1592 the Portuguese carrack and treasure ship *Madre de Dios* which was returning from her second voyage to the East Indies was intercepted close to Spain by a fleet of four English privateers, the *Dainty, Roebuck, Golden Dragon,* and the Queen's ship the *Foresight,* all under the command of Sir John Burrough. The great carrack weighed 1,600tons (of which 900 were cargo) – three times the size of England's biggest ship. She was 165ft long and 47ft beam, seven storeys high and had 32 brass cannons. The battle was fierce as the four manoeuvrable privateers encircled her, pounding the huge towering stern and repeatedly creating carnage among the 12 to 14 men needed to handle her huge tiller-steering. Finally, boarding parties brought her downfall and Burrough showed compassion allowing the Spanish captain Don Fernando de Mendosa and most of his crew to make for the nearby Spanish coast.

Among the riches were chests filled with jewels and pearls, gold and silver coins, amber, rolls of the highest-quality cloth, fine tapestries, 425 tons of pepper, 45 tons of cloves, 35 tons of cinnamon, 3 tons of mace and 3 of nutmeg, 2.5 tons of benjamin (a highly aromatic balsamic resin used for perfumes and medicines), 25 tons of cochineal and 15 tons of ebony. The English crews, mainly west-country men, stuffed their pockets full of these goods before their squadron commander, Sir John Burrough, could take charge of the cargo. Much of this found its way in small boats to various west-country ports where it 'disappeared'.

A Carrack typical of the era

The *Madre de Dios* was then brought to the Dart arriving 7 September. The carrack attracted all manner of traders, dealers, cutpurses and thieves from miles around, and even from as far as London and beyond; they visited the floating castle and sought out drunken sailors in taverns and pubs, buying, stealing, pinching and fighting for the takings. Local fishermen as well would constantly venture aboard and back to shore, further depleting the cargo.

English law at the time provided that a large share of the treasure was owed to the sovereign. Looting had got out of hand and when Queen Elizabeth found out what was happening, she sent Sir Walter Raleigh to reclaim her money and punish the looters. At that time Raleigh was imprisoned in the tower for marrying the Queen's handmaiden, Elisabeth Throckmorton, without the Queen's permission.

Because of his local west-country popularity, and as he had been a substantial contributor to the cost of the expedition, he was released but with Cecil as minder accompanying him, to recover any stolen property. Raleigh swore, *If I meet any of them coming up, if it be upon the wildest heath in all the way, I mean to strip them as naked as they were ever born, for Her Majesty has been robbed and that of the most rare things.*

They had some success and during Raleigh's brief period of liberty there was a touching meeting between Raleigh and his half-brother from Greenway, Sir John Gilbert.

By the time Raleigh had restored order a cargo estimated at half a million pounds, nearly half the size of England's treasury, had been reduced to less than one third. Ten ships were then loaded with the *Madre de Dios*'s remaining treasure and sailed around the coast from the Dart and up the River Thames to London where the contents were officially valued at Leadenhall at the then astonishing figure of £140,000.

The great ship remained in the Dart, but its sheer size, maintenance and huge crew requirements even in those days meant that for private enterprise she had no commercial value for trading. So she was stripped of her timbers, and the ribbed skeleton slowly rotted away and disintegrated into the mud and quiet waters of the Dart.

> To capitalise on her bounty Queen Elizabeth rigged the pepper market in 1592. When her 3,652 bags of pepper reached London there was such a quantity that no one merchant could be found to buy it all. The Queen owned the largest quantity, her share being worth 80,000 pounds, and Richard Carwarden, a great merchant of those days, was instructed by Lord Burghley to ask three shillings a pound for it.
>
> At the same time the city authorities were warned that no other pepper was to be placed on the market until the Queen's lot had been sold. It was eventually sold to Mr. Garraway for more than the sum stipulated, but this glut of the spice caused such a drop in prices that a few months later a warrant was issued by the Queen, prohibiting all importation of pepper for one year or longer, according to the Lord Treasurer's discretion. Of course difficulties arose and certain merchants were quickly charged under the warrant with importing pepper contrary to regulations.
>
> The whole situation seems somewhat undignified, as presenting a spectacle of the Queen and her courtiers quarrelling over plunder gained from Spain by what was after all brazen piracy.

3 1852 a lighter sinks

The *Exeter Flying Post*, 16 December 1852, reported that the PS *Undine* on passage from Totnes to Dartmouth ran into an empty lighter in the dark. The lighter was sunk with the loss of skipper Giles Shinner. Blame was attributed to the lighter not carrying lights in spite of being cautioned many times previously.

4 1855 *FLOATING BRIDGE No 1* the higher ferry

Built in 1831 in Plymouth, she sank in a storm in 1855 at her Sandquay moorings, and as Sir Henry Paul Seale made no moves to replace her, a legal writ forced him to raise her. She was towed to W Kelly's Sandquay yard, and there was stripped down to her bare frame, then partly restructured by the yard foreman Mr Mansfield, and clad with timbers from the Mount Boone estate. In 1856 she returned to service as *Floating Bridge No 2* with a steam capstan replacing the horse, and later she was replaced by a steam ferry in 1867.

Floating Bridge No I *powered by a horse-driven capstan*
Tom Casey/Don Collinson

1856 was the port's most charismatic year ever, due to the following chronicle of events:

1 Mr William Shaw Lindsey, an entrepreneurial ship-owner and winner of the Government contract for taking the royal mail to the Cape and Colonies, chose Kingswear in Dartmouth harbour as the port of departure. The SS *England* became the first liner departing from the port.

2 Two new paddle steamers rivalling each other, Holdsworth's *Dartmouth* and Seale Hayne's *Louisa,* began a river service to Totnes.

3 Queen Victoria with Prince Albert and the royal family visited for the second time. Aboard the Royal Yacht *Victoria & Albert II* they sailed into the harbour on Dartmouth Regatta day. Later the royal party steamed up-river aboard the *Dartmouth*, and before leaving Her Majesty allowed Dartmouth the honour of affixing the title 'Royal' to all future regattas.

4 The foundation stone for the harbour's Dartmouth Castle Lighthouse was laid by Mr Charles Seale Hayne.

5 Mr Charles Seale Hayne and seventy-seven prominent citizens called a public meeting to discuss the creation of railway communication to Dartmouth.

5 1856 *HUBERTUS* a Prussian brig

On 17 February 1856, the Prussian brig *Hubertus* of Stetten, with J Lehmen as master, and on passage from Newcastle to Bordeaux was laden with coal and when working through the Narrows a buffeting wind caused sternway, swinging her heel on to the flat rock known as Castle Foot. With the wind dead on-shore she then swung round striking heavily on the adjacent Castle Rocks and began filling with water which at high tide covered her. It was feared she would break up so her stores were recovered and her sails and rigging secured. On the following day her yards and top-masts were got down and her lower masts cut away to relieve the pressure. However, labouring heavily on the rocks on each tide, her bottom was driven in and her cargo of coals began to wash out onto the adjacent shoreline and into Warfleet Creek. Soon large numbers of men women and children were searching for the heaven-sent 'black diamonds'. On the 22 March the wreck was sold at auction for £60 to Sandquay shipbuilder Mr Kelly who tried to re-float her with casks, but later the port pilots got her off and floated her to Mr Kelly's Sandquay dock. After purchasing her sails, yards and masts at the New Ground auction, he rebuilt her.

Meanwhile, local confidence was at an all time high as the port had become a Mail Station for the Cape and Colonies. The Dartmouth lighthouse had been built and steamers were departing monthly, but regrettably the mail-ships were underpowered and were failing to maintain the Government schedules. So after barely a year's operation, the contract was terminated.

However, during 1857 good progress had been made with Charles Seale Hayne's ambitious scheme to link the harbour to the country's ever-growing railway system. The Dartmouth and Torbay Railway Co had been formed, funds raised, a Parliamentary Bill approved, Isambard Kingdom Brunel appointed as engineer, the route surveyed, estimates obtained, a contractor appointed, ground bought, and an official start made in January 1858.

6 1858 *MERIT* a Brixham smack

In May the *Chronicle* reported another shipwreck which fortunately involved no loss of life. While entering harbour the sloop *Merit* owned by Mr Thomas Moses was short-handed having lent a man to a vessel awaiting a pilot; she was caught by contrary winds which drove her onto the rocks below Kingswear Castle. The remaining four crewmen got safely ashore by dinghy but as the sloop was holed, she filled with water and remained affixed on the rocks. She had been Brixham-built only four months previously by Messrs Dewdney at a cost of £780, and was insured with the Brixham Fishing Society for £300. The president of the society Mr G Buckingham, and the committee took it on themselves to patch and raise the wreck on a rising tide with the aid of four other sloops affixed two per side. They were successful, and she was run up on the beach adjacent to Kingswear's Lower Ferry Slip and Mr Avis's boatyard for later repair.

7 1861 Last of the **TOTNES PACKET BOATS**

In 1861 a local tragedy occurred when the last surviving Totnes packet boat sank, causing the death of the master Robert Kelland who had 47 years experience. Previously, numerous Totnes passage boats — 35/40ft gaff-rigged ketches — had carried both passengers and cargo to and from Totnes, but after the introduction in 1836 of the paddle-driven steamships, the sailing ketches lost their trade to the steamships.

As the Dartmouth Steam Packet Co tug *Pilot* was returning to Dartmouth, she offered Robert Kelland a tow which was gratefully accepted. Kelland unfortunately had at the wheel an inexperienced helmsman who at a turn in the river allowed the packet boat to drop athwart the wash caused by the tug's paddles. She over-turned, the tow rope broke and she sank. The helmsman was saved by hanging on to a crate but Mr Kelland was not found until the following day. As the old packet boat was severely damaged, she was written off and left to moulder away on the river bank at Parkers Barn bend in Totnes.

8 1862 *MALEYER* a Dutch barque

On 17 January 1862 the *Maleyer*, Captain Bok, from West Hartlepool bound for Batavia (now Jakarta) with steam coal had been towed into the harbour and was anchored in The Bight. The mate, returning in the early hours, smelled fire; he alerted the captain and the crew who battened down the hatches, and he contacted harbour master Mr Tipper, the coastguard and the revenue cruiser *Wickham*. Fortunately the tide was flooding so the anchors were weighed and the ship run ashore onto the mud banks above Hoodown. The captain's and the crew's goods were removed to the Customs House, while the fire in the cargo gained hold, so a hole was made in her bow and she filled with water.

The sails were unbent and stored on the pilot sloop *Fanny* while the yards, top hamper and rigging were cut away and large scuttle holes cut low in her sides to allow water to flow into the hull as the tide rose. However, being listed over, a large part of her cargo was clear of water so the coals burned and by late evening she was a mass of flames from stem to stern. Attempts were made to cut across the deck to save a portion of the ship, but to no avail and with spectators gathered at Sandquay to watch the disaster, the fire burned all night. Finally all the masts went over the side, everything being consumed to the waterline. The fire illuminated the night sky causing people to ride miles to see the disaster.

The next few years were to be the port's halcyon days, for after six and a half years' construction the railway finally arrived at Kingswear, the Dart Harbour Commission was formed, and more steamships were calling for bunkering. Fortunately, during those years the harbour remained free from mishap.

1866 THE GREAT GALE

In 1866, only ten days into the New Year, gales of hurricane force struck Torbay, but fortunately Dartmouth was on the fringe of the storm and missed the main fury of the tempest with little more than a few small craft sinking. Sadly out of the 79 vessels sheltering in Torbay, only eleven rode out the gale, and over 100 lives were lost. Eight vessels driven ashore were

The aftermath of the Great Gale in Brixham 1866 *Dartmouth Museum*

got off, and several other wrecks had to be sold where they lay. Some could have made the safety of Brixham harbour but for a number of trawlers that were moored directly in the entrance and with which they fouled, losing control of their vessels.

Out of this misfortune the Dartmouth Steam Packet Company's steam tug *Pilot* had its most lucrative period ever, being engaged night and day for months on numerous salvage operations.

9 1868 *ALEXANDER II* a paddle steamer, later *William & Thomas*

In late 1867 a new company, Messrs Chennals, challenged the Dartmouth Steam Packet Company for supremacy on the Dart by forming the Totnes Saloon Company. They purchased at very low cost from the Alexander Saloon Co (a failed London company), the *Alexander II,* 147×17×2ft3in with a 60ft long saloon, and licensed to carry 400 passengers.

The paddle steamer *Alexander II* later renamed the *William & Thomas* entered service in 1868 but proved impractical for the River Dart. The Sunday service had lacked support, the steering proved difficult and she was running into other vessels, her paddle-boxes became damaged by grounding and inefficient handling which caused much rock damage to her paddles. All this frequently caused the passengers to demand to be put ashore to make their own return. Finally she tore her plates and so limped into an inlet near Bow Creek and was left to disintegrate.

10 1868 *MARINUS* the first standing hulk

Mr Armeson, who in 1866 had returned from India, seized an opportunity to advance the bunkering of calling steamships. Instead of the smaller shifting hulks used by the present supplier, he used *Marinus* as a sizeable moored standing hulk, alongside which coaling vessels could tie up.

He purchased the brig *Marinus* previously grounded off Berry Head and had her towed round by the tug *Pilot* to the New Ground for repair. Then he stationed her off Hoodown, Kingswear, but unfortunately she broke her moorings and ran up on the rocks at One Gun Point, below the house Gunfield, and because of his many other commitments – trawling, contracting, and the Sandquay Brickworks – he left her to disintegrate.

Marinus *alongside the New Ground, Dartmouth*

Standing hulks became standard five years later and had he persisted he would have been the fore-runner of the port's lucrative coaling trade which continued for a further eighty-five years.

11 1870 *EUREKA* a brig

During January, the *Eureka*, 240 tons and less than a year old, while carrying coals Newcastle to Devonport was hit by mountainous seas when off Portland. This made her cargo shift causing a heavy list to starboard. Then a wind change carried her down channel and forced her to make for Dartmouth harbour. Unfortunately on 6 February when off the Mewstone, she was driven onto the rocks at outer Froward Point where sadly three men were drowned, but two scrambled ashore and scaled the cliff face to reach the safety of Brownstone Farm.

12 1870 *COURSER* a schooner

In February the Brixham schooner *Courser*, Fécamp to Torbay, while in ballast for orders encountered severe gales near the Western Blackstone and lost her main-sail. She dropped her anchor which began to drag and so they hoisted distress signals, but before the Dartmouth tug *Guide* could make contact, she drove ashore onto the rocks by the harbour mouth and quickly began to break up. So Captain Brusey and the five crew members took to the boat and tried to make for the *Guide* but they overturned. By now numerous spectators lined the shore and saw five of the men drown in the bitterly cold water, but one man was washed close in and was saved by the gallant action of the brother of the landlord of the Royal Oak Inn (next to Agincourt House), who at great peril waded out and seized the man, hauling him ashore.

These two tragedies in two months renewed calls for a lifeboat, or at least life-saving apparatus to be stationed in the River, but there were to be other tragedies and a further eight years before the calls were answered.

Mr R L Hingston, the main local bunkering agent, who eight years previously had purchased from W Ashford the original Dartmouth bunkering company (founded in 1855), adopted Mr Armeson's concept of using a standing hulk which enabled steamers to tie up alongside for coaling, and in his capacity as French Consul he purchased and adapted the condemned 300ton French brig *Happy* for use as the harbour's first standing hulk.

Contrary to the old poem

Oh, River of Dart, Oh, River of Dart,
Every year thou claim a heart

the river claimed none for the next three years but in August 1875 a shipping casualty occurred in the harbour that could have had serious implications.

13 1875 *SENSATION* a Teignmouth steamer

Messrs Wards of Teignmouth had two steamers which made regular excursions to Torbay and Dartmouth, and on 7 August 1878 the *Sensation* with over 150 on board went aground at Torbay; this delayed her arrival at Dartmouth until after eight o'clock. The weather was calm and a thick fog enshrouded the harbour entrance. The passengers landed and after an hour re-embarked. In spite of the fog, now even thicker, *Sensation* proceeded at nearly full speed down the harbour hugging the Kingswear shore. She had no regular pilot aboard and was steered by a lad of little experience.

In the fog she ran stem first onto the rocks of the Inner Froward Ledge and stuck fast. The cries of the passengers through the fog were pitiful and attracted the attention of Mr McQuire, Kingswear Lighthouse keeper, a nearby steam ship and a yacht anchored in The Bight. They contacted the coastguard who with two galleys of Mr Avis, Kingswear boat builder, and boats from the Naval College they rowed hard in the direction of the cries, but because of the thick fog they had great difficulty in locating the vessel. Finally Mr Lyons, coastguard chief boatman, made contact and got aboard restoring order among the panic-stricken passengers. He then allowed the boats to come alongside and first took off the women and children, then the men, and all were landed at various points in the harbour.

Some found accommodation in hotels and private residences, while others slept in empty railway carriages at the station. All made their way back to Teignmouth by train on the following morning.

The *Sensation* was recovered but served little thereafter and was soon sold away for disposal. She was replaced by the 1852 tug *Pilot,* an 84ft iron paddle steamer which Messrs Wards purchased from the River Dart Steamboat Co.

Because of this incident the case for the harbour to have a lifeboat was now progressed with increased vigour and the Royal National Lifeboat Institute agreed that due to the danger caused by the increasing number and size of steamships calling for bunkers, one should be stationed in the harbour. Messrs Pillar of Dartmouth secured the tender for constructing a lifeboat building at Sandquay. The vessel was presented by Mrs Emma Hargreaves of Cleygate, Surrey and named *Maud Hargreaves* in memory of her late daughter. She was built by Wolfe & Son, of Poplar, London, and tested out on the Limehouse Canal.

In October 1878 the new lifeboat arrived by rail at Kingswear terminus. She was a 33ft long by 8ft beam, ten-oared intermediate and self-righting and discharging vessel. She was towed over to the New Ground, hauled ashore and placed on the launching slip provided by Messrs Redway Shipbuilders. After a sizeable parade of dignitaries around the town behind the Britannia Band, with great ceremony she was launched by Mrs Hockin, with her captain Mr Lewis and her crew aboard. They pulled round HMS *Britannia* which was moored in the Dart, and on returning, to the cheers of the crowd rescued a twelve year old boy who had fallen into the harbour.

14 1878 *COMET* a schooner

In November the schooner *Comet*, bound Sligo to London with oats, pulled into the Range with a split mainsail and broken fore-gaff, and anchored in the Narrows by Kingswear Castle close to Mill Bay Cove. The tug *Hauley*, noticing her dangerous position, warned her, but they refused a tow and when trying to re-set the mainsail she missed stays and drifted shorewards. She then dropped her anchor which failed to hold, and because of low water the tug was unable to get a line aboard. *Comet* was washed onto the rocks and began to break up, later becoming a total wreck; fortunately the crew managed to scramble over the rocks and scale the cliff face to the shelter of Mr Charles Seale Hayne's Brownstone Farm, occupied by Mr Nutes.

For the next two years there were no calamities in the harbour and after all the years of local campaigning for Dartmouth to be made a Lifeboat Station, the following decade of the eighties proved to be one of tranquillity.

However for oysterman Mr Eli Fleet, fortune smiled, for when fishing off Brookhill he netted an ivory elephant tusk 5ft9in long. Over the years several have been recovered there, being part of the booty of a privateer which, when anchored in The Bight over two hundred years previously, burned to the waterline and sank at her moorings.

15 1882 *PRODOMO* a Norwegian barque

On 11 May 1882, a series of events in the harbour was enacted which instead of having the hallmarks of tragedy that usually accompany a wreck, had all the making of a stage comedy. The principal character was the Norwegian barque *Prodomo*, bound Rotterdam to New York with a general cargo. In the

English Channel she collided with SS *Bayswater* in ballast, bound Antwerp to Cardiff. The barque began to take in water so the steamer took her in tow for nearby Dartmouth harbour.

Fortunately, as she was settling fast, they met the Dartmouth tug *Hauley* which took over the tow. With great difficulty they worked her though the Narrows between the two castles, and ran her up on the beach below Kingswear Lighthouse, where the action began.

Principal players: Messrs Bartlett & Coleman, salvage contractors of Whitstable, Kent. A large audience gathers to see the show.

Act One – Recovery in a Week

June 2 Divers make good the damage and holes, some powerful pumps are placed on board, some cargo removed and placed in store.

June 9 She is pumped out and raised four feet and floats, but shows signs of heeling into deep water, so 2,000 coils of steel wire are removed. She then re-settles in deep water.

June 16 A new steam pump discharges five tons of water per minute. She rises and floats but then the pump breaks down and she settles again.

June 23 Pumping again. She rises this time until her coppered bow is visible but more coils of wire (missed by divers) are exposed. Then unexpectedly she settles again.

June 30 Forty tons more cargo are removed with further patching to the hull and confidence for a final lift next week.

July 7 Another attempt and she rises again, then heels over and water pours down the fore hatchway, causing the remaining cargo to shift to starboard. She sinks again. Mr Emmet, landlord of Kings Arms Hotel, Dartmouth, standing on the forecastle, is thrown into the water but is rescued by the divers.

So the Prodomo *was beached for three months at Lighthouse Cove, Kingswear, and was supposed to be raised within a week but she actually was raised and settled seven times.*

Sept 8 She is raised and stays afloat, towed across the harbour and is finally anchored to a buoy off the New Ground.

Interval

After three months the Norwegian consul George Henry Collins, the largest bunkering agent in the harbour, is commissioned to dispose of the vessel and her cargo.

Finale – A Sleight of Hand

Oct 13 Numerous people attend the sale and the cargo makes a good price. The masts and rigging are sold separately and the hull is purchased by Mr Colney, of Plymouth, for £250.

It turns out that Mr Colney is a nominee purchaser to hide the identity of the real buyer Mr R L Hingston, a Dartmouth coal bunkering agent and rival to Mr Collins. Hingston's business is in decline because his main standing hulk, the old 300ton Happy *is dwarfed by Collins' 1,180ton hulk* Monarch. *So the acquisition of the 600ton* Prodomo *puts Hingston's business on a more equal footing, and she serves for several more years before being run ashore at Ballast Cove, Kingswear. Like so many once-proud ships, but now worn-out coal hulks, she finally rots away.*

****

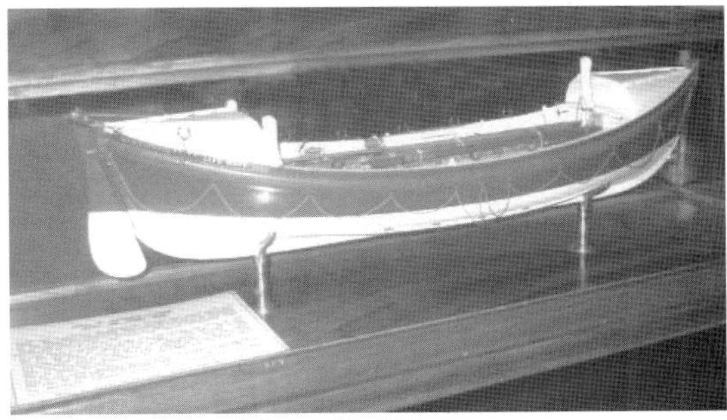

The Henry and Amanda Shaw
Dartmouth Museum

In 1887 the ten oared Dartmouth lifeboat *Maude Hargreaves*, after an uneventful ten year stint without having once attended a wreck or saved a life, was replaced by a new twelve-oared lifeboat, the *Henry and Amanda Shaw*, 34ft×8ft London built and self-righting. Strangely her required services were also minimal over the following years and regrettably seemed to inspire little local support.

MODEL OF DARTMOUTH LIFEBOAT
"HENRY AND AMANDA SHAW"

There was a lifeboat at Dartmouth between the years 1878 and 1896. The "Henry and Amanda Shaw", the second of the two boats on the Dartmouth station. was ceremonially launched at Sandquay by her donor Mrs Shaw of Exeter in 1887. The boat was 33ft long and was of the self-righting, water ballasted type propelled by oars and sails.

Of the three occasions on which she was called out only on one did she assist in the rescue of a vessel in distress. This was on the morning of January 11th, 1894. The Brixham ketch "Prince of Wales" was stranded near Kingswear Castle. The lifeboat left her moorings at 10.45. Meanwhile a tug had taken the stricken vessel in tow and was heading back to the harbour when the lifeboaat arrived. Four Dartmouth lifeboatmen were able to board her and assisted at the pumps and one hour later she was safely beached.

During the summer months the lifeboat was housed at Sandquay in what is now the Dartmouth Rowing Club. In the winter the boat was kept at moorings in Warfleet Creek.

The Dartmouth lifeboat service was discontinued in 1896.

16 1888 *BERRY CASTLE I* and *DARTMOUTH CASTLE I* paddle steamers

In 1880 the *Berry Castle I* was built at Polyblank's yard in Waterhead Creek, Kingswear. She was manoeuvred under the railway bridge and finished at Philips, Sandquay. For nearly twenty years she ran a daily service to and from Totnes. In 1888 at 10pm on 8 August she went aground near Dittisham in fog with 200 passengers.

PS Berry Castle *fully laden on the daily round trip service Dartmouth to Totnes*

The first *Dartmouth Castle I* which together with the *Berry Castle* provided two round trips Dartmouth/Totnes daily went to assist but also went aground and both had to wait until the following day to re-float without serious damage.

Steamers and the River Dart Steamboat Co Ltd

Prior to the 1830s, shipping and trade from the sea could not go up stream beyond Sharpham and sea-borne goods were carried further up by a fleet of nearly fifty lighters. The Duke of Somerset around 1834 dredged and improved the upper reaches enabling steam driven vessels to proceed to Totnes. In 1836 the first steamer was the *Dart* a three masted lugger rigged paddle steamer running a daily passenger and goods service Dartmouth to Totnes with stops in between. From 1848 Totnes train passengers were carried and in 1865 the railway reached Kingswear. For many years a twice daily summer service was continued calling at Dittisham, Greenway and Duncannon latterly by the River Dart Steamboat Coy. Since 1880 there have been three *Dartmouth Castles*, three *Berry Castles*, two *Totnes Castles*, two *Kingswear Castles*, and six other *Castles*.

In the 1940s change was inevitable, for the proposed nationalisation of the railway system would be carried through. Increasing costs meant the River Dart's ageing fleet of paddle steamers had problems, being broad-beamed, of shallow draft, with little carrying capacity, heavy on coal and demanding of personnel. So it was obvious that the RDSB's fleet, when not doing service for the river's American WWII forces, would have to lie up for the duration of the war.

The traditional RDSC Dart steamer was a paddle driven boat of about 100ft and of their boats:

PS *Dartmouth Castle II* (see No.56, page 38) (built by Cox, Falmouth, 1907) during the war was berthed at the company's Creekside Boatyard in Old Mill Creek, and still acts as a retaining wall.

The Kingswear Castle II *in Old Mill Creek lying alongside the paddle-wheels and remains of* Dartmouth Castle II *J B Millar*

PS *Compton Castle* (built by Cox, Falmouth, 1914), PS *Totnes Castle II* (see No.57, page 38) (built by Philips, Dartmouth, 1923) and *Kingswear Castle II* (built by Philips, Dartmouth, 1924) were laid up during the war in the river outside the company's workshops at Hoodown Point

In 1963 the PS *Compton Castle* was withdrawn and finally, after some time at Kingsbridge, ended her days as a heavily mutilated hull serving as a restaurant near Truro, Cornwall. She had served during the war as an ammunition transport vessel in the river.

The only one still sailing today is PS *Kingswear Castle II*; she was built in 1924 by Philips and worked on the river until WWII when she served as a store ship and tender to the US forces. In 1965 she was restored by the Paddle Steamer Preservation Society and is currently in service in Medway, coal fired and paddle driven. Her engine, still serving, is the one removed from *Kingswear Castle I* (see No.36, page 28) and which has served both so well since 1904.

But in recent times as roads and personal transport have developed further, the river boats' role has become merely to provide excursions for the holiday making public.

17 1890 *AMITY* a cutter

The harbour was free from tempest until 19 September 1890. In a strong gale the cutter *Amity* of Dittisham, laden with a full cargo of sand, was making for Torquay when a freak wind drove her hard and fast on the rocks at Kettle Cove, Kingswear. Soon she broke open and at high water only the mast remained visible. The master/owner was not insured.

18 1893 *THEKLA* tragedy

On 14 January 1893 a German ship the *Thekla* arrived off Dartmouth harbour in passage from Iquique bound for Hamburg. She was short of provisions and called for a pilot from the pilot sloop *Gwendoline* which was sailing in the Range. Pilot Coaker was transferred to the *Thekla.* The harbour gig of Fox, Sons and Co came out from the port to take the *Thekla's* captain ashore to get the provisions.

The wind had increased from the east with a strong ebb tide and George Macey, local boarding clerk and manager of Fox's, was begged without success not to take the Captain and his provisions back out in the gig, but to hire a tug. Regardless, the gig in the charge of Mr Macey with four rowers James Stevens, John Collins, George Lidster and Edward Lidster returned the Captain to *Thekla* which was 'dodging' about under sail in the care of pilot Coaker about three miles off the harbour mouth. *Gwendoline* had returned to the harbour but the pilot cutter *Rose,* manned by pilot William Kelland and extra-men Gurney and Joseph Maycock, came out to pick up Coaker who had joined the five men in the gig. It had become much more rough with a heavy easterly gale and *'Snow began to fall very thickly a few minutes before five and, with the howling and shrieking of the keen biting wind and the foaming and raging of the sea, combined to make the scene at once wild and weird'.*

The cutter *Rose* was hove-to upwind of the gig for the transfer but was hit by a violent squall which swept over them laying the cutter on her beam ends. She was deluged by the waves, becoming quite unmanageable, and as the bow fell off, the bowsprit plunged and drove into the gig lifting it clean out of the water and throwing all six men into the sea. Only pilot Coaker was picked up by seizing a rope flung to him by Gurney. As soon as Coaker was on board, pilot Kelland and Gurney launched the cutter's boat and proceeded in search of the drowning men of whom nothing was afterwards seen or heard. Pilot Coaker and extra-man Maycock were the only hands left on board the *Rose* and it was some time, with the gig hanging suspended on the bowsprit, before the cutter was fairly manageable. It was dark, snowing and a full gale, with visibility about forty yards; the masthead light blew out and it was not possible to keep any flares alight. The cutter *Rose* searched for some time for Kelland and Gurney but it was clear that the two men in an open rowing boat and against gale and tide would be unable to get back to the river entrance. In spite of searching, and being joined by the Dartmouth lifeboat which had come out under coxswain Pillar, no sign was found of the *Rose's* boat or the gig's five lost men.

In fact Kelland and Gurney managed to get ashore at Blackpool where they were picked up by a coach searching for them and returned to Dartmouth. In the calamity five young local men had lost their lives in spite of the great courage shown by pilots Coaker and Kelland, and extra-man Gurney.

RNLI Silver to Wm R KELLAND)

19 1896 *PENDENNIS* a steam tug

The owners Renwick & Wilton Co Ltd mainly supplied house coals over Kingswear's quays with their colliers *Sabrina, Mezzeppa,* and *Vanessa*. In 1894, prior to entering the local bunkering trade, they purchased the Falmouth-built tug *Pendennis* 35tons, 81ft long. In 1895 *Pendennis* caught fire but with their launch *Kingswear* they were able to tow her inshore where she sank. Philips managed to raise her and carried out extensive repairs but sadly in 1896 she was again engulfed in flames and sank. This time the company abandoned her.

Pendennis , *Kingswear Quay in background*
Dartmouth Museum

Early in 1896 the Royal National Lifeboat Institute decided that the lifeboat station would be better placed elsewhere. They closed it down in spite of Dartmouth being at its zenith for steamers calling for bunkers, and being the largest coal bunkering station on the south coast. In the twenty years service of the two lifeboats, the station had received little local support and was criticised for incompetence and inefficiency. They had been called out three times only once reaching a vessel, had performed no rescues, had once failed to muster, and had saved no lives. But hardly had the lifeboat been withdrawn when in May 1898 the sea moved in triumph.

20 1898 *LETITIA* a schooner

During a strong south west gale the 96ton schooner *Letitia* with Captain Towes, while on passage from Poole to Runcorn with a cargo of clay, was seen in difficulties making for Dartmouth harbour. The wind was baffling and two hundred yards off Kingswear Castle she missed stays and let the anchor go to ride stem on to the huge waves. Captain Pillar from the tug *Hauley* rowed out, but failed to get a hawser aboard. When *Letitia*'s anchor cables parted, a huge wave carried away her rudder, and washed her into Mill Bay Cove and onto the ragged rocks. A boat was launched but immediately capsized flinging a crewman into the water. After a desperate struggle, he got close enough to the high-water mark where two Kingswear men bravely rushed in to rescue him.

Meanwhile the coastguards had rowed across from Dartmouth and managed to get aboard, and with ropes they rigged up a shore lifeline by which the crew were got safely ashore. The mate and two coastguards found the captain 'dead of a fit' on the cabin floor. With difficulty and the help of men from the various coaling companies who had by now arrived, they got his body up and ashore and conveyed it to Kingswear mortuary. The crew were kindly received at Glenlorleigh, (today Kingswear Court) and by the following morning the *Letitia* had broken up.

21 1903 *GALATEA* an America's Cup contender

In 1903 a freak storm interrupted a run of reasonable weather.

Lt and Mrs Henn's Galatea

Yachting World 1894

One of the recently arrived large French trawlers in the harbour broke her moorings and became a maverick causing mayhem among the many other anchored vessels in the harbour. First she collided with the schooner *Ella* bringing down her fore and topmasts, then choosing sterner metal she rammed head on into Sir George Jackson's large salvage dredger *Zeppa*. From there she turned and crashed into the salvage hopper, and broadside on struck Mrs Henn's beautiful yacht *Galatea*, a former America's Cup contender. The trawler, badly damaged, ran aground in Ballast Cove.

Mrs Henn was a remarkable lady who in 1877 married Lt W Henn RN of County Clare; both came from wealthy backgrounds. In 1884 they issued a challenge in *Galatea* in an attempt to be the first British yacht to win the America's Cup which had remained with the Americans since it was first won off the Isle of Wight in 1851. Sadly in 1886 they lost. Mrs Henn was the first woman ever to have sailed a racing yacht across the Atlantic, and she and her husband continued living in luxury aboard *Galatea* in the harbour. Lt Henn died in 1894 but Mrs Henn remained on *Galatea* dying on board in 1911. Unfortunately the above incident had caused her to relocate her mooring to the broader waters of Plymouth Sound. *Galatea* was broken up the year following Mrs Henn's death.

Turmoil in the harbour over the next few years was matched by the long-term in-fighting of the local harbour coaling owners endeavouring to establish individual supremacy. They later joined temporarily to create a united front to deny another coaling factor a berth in the harbour. This proved to be a costly miscalculation for the same company approached the Brixham Harbour Commissioners, who gladly gave it permission to establish there a rival competing coaling station; it was a mere five miles from Dartmouth. This state of affairs continued until the early twenties when the Brixham and Dartmouth companies were all absorbed and amalgamated by Cardiff entrepreneur Cdr C H Evans, who transformed both harbours into the biggest coal consortium on the South Coast.

The coaling companies' area in the harbour extended along the Kingswear shoreline from above Noss through Ballast Cove to Hoodown Point. Here numerous once-proud ships were anchored to act as either standing or shifting hulks in order to serve their coal to the younger calling steamships for voyages to the four corners of the world. The hulks' tour of duty ranged from a few years to twenty or more and thereafter they were either abandoned at Ballast Cove for breaking up, or towed away to a breaker's yard.

22 1905 *ARETHUSA* a whaling ship

The old whaling ship *Arethusa*, which was touring the country's harbours and was used as a floating museum, had arrived in Dartmouth. In her hold was a preserved 72ft stuffed whale along with sharks and other strange creatures of the deep. It was moored in the Coombe Inlet, and admission was sixpence from Mr Adams, boatman, on The Quay.

Misfortune overtook the vessel when she sprang a leak and sank at her moorings. So the 72ft whale, caught in 1903 near Spitzbergen, with all the other species aboard, were for a short period returned to their natural habitat.

In late February Philips of Sandquay managed to raise the *Arethusa,* and her German owners with their tug *Neufahrwasser* then towed her to Hamburg. The exhibits were given to a museum and the *Arethusa* broken up. Fresh exhibits were to be acquired and a new ship bought for travelling exhibitions in continental ports.

23 1906 *TRY* a ketch

On 18 September the ketch *Try* of Goole carrying stone for Plymouth encountered ferocious winds off Portland and in Lyme Bay and was forced to make for Dartmouth. When approaching the Range a split mainsail resulted in her being driven onto rocks at the Eastern Blackstone. Fortunately Renwick and Wilton's tug *Victor* was in the harbour mouth and on seeing *Try*'s predicament she closed in. With great difficulty *Victor* got a line aboard and after several hours, managed on the rising tide to free her and tow her into the shelter of the harbour. She was damaged and minus her anchors and ship's boat, but was repaired and some weeks later was able to continue her journey.

24 1910 *ELIZABETH* a Plymouth smack

Renwick and Wilton tug Totnes
Dartmouth Museum

Having delivered her cargo of sand, the smack *Elizabeth* was making for her home port, Plymouth. In mid-channel severe weather drove her towards Dartmouth, so they decided to make for the harbour. Unfortunately in the Range she collided with the stern of the pilot cutter causing her to lose her headgear and drift towards the Kingswear Castle rocks. Unable to control the vessel, the crew abandoned ship and boarded the cutter. The smack was driven onto the rocks and stove in, despite the efforts of the tug *Totnes* to save her.

25 1910 *MORNING STAR* a Brixham trawler

Morning Star was built in 1897 by Dewdney as DH148 but re-registered in 1906 as BM183. On 14 October after battling with fierce storms throughout the day *Morning Star* made for the shelter of Dartmouth harbour and dropped anchor abreast of Kingswear Castle. The following morning the Renwick & Wilton tug *Totnes* saw the vessel sheering dangerously and there was no one on deck. Then a man appeared and quickly asked for a tow. The tug requested they shorten the anchor chain to reduce the sheering, but they over shortened it and as the trawler began to drift to the rocks all the crew boarded their boat and made for the tug with a tow rope that proved too short. When the tug offered their tow-rope, the crew said they had no thole pins to row back; so the trawler went aground on Kettle Rock, became holed and settled in six fathoms.

Her crew were all saved and later she was sold, her booms and rigging were removed, her masts cut away, and her hulk raised. She was towed to Warfleet Creek where she was stripped of her timbers, and rotted away.

Morning Star *abandoned in Warfleet Creek*
Postcard

26 1912 *DAISY* a Dittisham barge

In October 1912, after encountering bad weather in the Range, the Dittisham barge *Daisy* with a full load of sand, began to take water. She was steered towards the shore and struck the rocks by the white fairway light on the west side of the channel abreast of Sugary Cove. She sank in deep water, until only the top of her mast was showing. The two members of the crew fortunately were able to scramble ashore to the safety of the high ground. Later the Harbour Commission instructed divers to blow up the remains of the wreck.

27 1915 *ZEUS* a Dutch steamship

In late April the Dutch vessel SS *Zeus* pulled alongside the Channel Coaling Company's coaling hulk *Prince Arthur*, and observed flames rising from the hulk's forecastle. The *Zeus* immediately pulled away with her sirens blaring, which brought the local inhabitants out to see the evening sky lit with flames. The tug *Venture* and the water-boat *Water Lily* played hoses on the fire, thus saving a valuable wartime cargo of coal and the hulk *Prince Arthur* and possibly also the *Zeus* from becoming wrecks in Dartmouth harbour.

28 1916 *SABRINA* a depot ship

In November the worst storms in living memory resulted in extensive damage to shipping in the harbour and the sinking of the depot ship *Sabrina.*

On the night of 10 November, with waves of mountainous height riding down the harbour, and with the shrill howling of the wind and the blackness of the night, it seemed as though Bedlam had broken loose. The Australian steamer SS *Yankalilla* broke her warps from the buoys, so she let her anchors go and steamed all night to fight the wind and tide. Then the shifting hulk moored alongside her broke adrift and drove down onto the brigantine *Huntley* and carried away her fore top gallant topmast. *Yankalilla* then cleared her, but drove across the SS *Cumberland Hall* which also broke adrift and fouled the collier *Emma Minloss* and then bore across to ram the large standing hulk *Sabrina* which, with a full cargo of coal, sank at her mooring. Meanwhile three other coal hulks broke free from their moorings, one landing up and blocking the Kingswear Ferry Slip, the others riding up on Ballast Cove foreshore. At Sandquay, the *Floating Bridge* broke free and was borne up on the Kingswear Slip and gouged out her timbers, while numerous small sailing and rowing-craft were sunk or lost.

That would seem enough, but the storm continued in its ferocity throughout the night and, sad to report, the *Chronicle* continued with a further horrific report of the wreck and loss of crew.

29 1916 *PRINCESS OF THULE* a schooner

On the Sunday morning, the tempest continued with unabated ferocity and the schooner *Princess of Thule* 210tons, in ballast and with Captain Arthur Pincher on passage from Barfleur to Par, Cornwall, was seen attempting to make the harbour.

Later at the inquest, a graphic account of the tragedy was given by Mr A T Langley, Dartmouth coastguard observer.

The schooner was about a mile off land and abreast the coastguard station when she started to drag towards the Blackstone. In the heavy tumultuous sea and as she turned to get up more sail, a heavy sea caught her broadside on and knocked her onto her beam-end, then carried her level with The Warren, Kingswear. Her jib and mainsails blew to ribbons, her masts broke and she was flung onto the treacherous rocks below Kingswear Castle where she broke up, causing the loss of the five crew members.

In November 1920, a curious incident in Torbay occurred, involving the wreck of two reparation German destroyers, the *S24* and the *T189*. Contrary to the usual sad ending to shipwrecks, in this case along with a condemned English submarine they made a contribution to the advancement of Dartmouth and the town's well-being.

30 1920 *T189* and *S24* German torpedo-boat destroyers

Torpedo-Boat Destroyer T189 *aground on Roundham Head, in Torbay* *R Tully*

The first year of the 'roaring twenties' really lived up to its name, for in November a great gale swept across Torbay, which became the scene of much heroic effort to assist two reparation German destroyers *S24* and the *T189* which had broken free of their tow ropes, and finally gone ashore.

The German destroyers were en route from Cherbourg to Teignmouth for breaking up. The Brixham lifeboat *Betsy Newbon II* (which almost capsized), Denaby and Cadeby's tug *Dencade*, and the smaller Dartmouth tugs endeavoured in vain to secure them before they were swept ashore at

Paignton. Fortunately the six-man steaming-crew aboard them had by then been transferred. One vessel came up on Roundham Point, the other on Preston slipway, and both were subsequently written off and sold. They were built in 1910, 220ft in length and cost over £40,000 each.

The *T189*, 646tons, lay in the more difficult position with her back broken on the rocks at Roundham Head, and made only £100. The *S24*, 555tons and in the more accessible position on Preston Beach made £545. They were bought by a Brixham man, Mr Shaw, who salvaged from the *T189* the more accessible parts, leaving the sea to claim the rest. However, in 1946 the bronze parts of the turbine engine and the propellers were recovered by an enterprising Kingswear man, the late Mr Jim Thorpe.

The *S24* was patched and towed to Brixham.

31 1920 an unnamed **BRITISH SUBMARINE**

Mr Shaw also purchased a condemned British submarine for £1,000, and for a charge opened up both the British submarine and one of the German destroyer hulls, *S24,* for public display before demolishing both down to the waterline.

Later the hulls of both vessels were towed to Dartmouth. As part of Dartmouth's programme of in-filling the Coombe Mud Inlet, they were hulked on the mud at right angles to each other opposite the Floating Bridge Inn, in order to act as a barrier to contain the creek in-filling which was being washed away into the main river. Both wrecks were thus finally buried under the infill behind the 1928/36 North Embankment extension which creates today's Coronation Park. Mr Shaw and his companions made sufficient out of the enterprise to retire and emigrate to Australia.

Looking South across Coombe Mud. The demolished hull of the British submarine and at right angles the bow of the German destroyer S24 *positioned as a retaining wall.*

R Jones/R Tucker

32 1921 SS *BROADMAYNE* a steam driven oil tanker

Another wreck occurred in the harbour, but this time the fault was not entirely due to Mother Nature but also to human error. An oil tank steamer had signalled for a pilot to guide her into the harbour, but because of the intensity of the storm the pilot boat could not make contact so the steamer proceeded without a pilot and with serious consequences for the vessel and all on board. She was the SS *Broadmayne* built in 1888 as the *Oka*. On New Year's Day 1921, in heavy weather and thick fog, the SS *Broadmayne*, 3,120 tons, was outward bound from London to Newport, Mass, and making for Dartmouth for bunkers. So the ship proceeded to enter, but failed to allow sufficient for lee-way and caught on the Castle Ledge buoy, breaking its cable which then twined around her propeller. Without her engines she was carried across the Range to run up on the rocks below Inner Froward Point.

The remaining bow and midship section of SS Broadmayne *showing the 'Mill folly' and Millbay Cove. She was towed there to be broken up and despatched by train from Kingswear.* *Dave Griffiths*

Then came a night of bravery. The Brixham lifeboat *Betsy Newbon II*, pulled by oarsmen, could not be launched until 2am because of the heavy weather and thick fog and was unable to reach the wreck until later in the morning. Meanwhile, Brixham Coxswain Sanders and Signalman Noraway with the aid of local Kingswear farmer Tom Bulley and his son, all on foot, located them. In the darkness Sanders climbed down the cliff face to find sixteen members of the crew who had scrambled ashore. With help the crew climbed the cliff face to safety, and those remaining aboard were advised to wait for the arrival of the lifeboat. The Brixham Rocket Brigade had made Herculean efforts to get their heavy wagon and equipment up to Hillhead, from where with the aid of three exhausted commandeered horses, they eventually reached the site, but unfortunately their rope ladders were too short to reach the rocks below. The lifeboat, after searching in the fog for six hours, finally saw a rocket fired from the vessel and moved in and rescued the remaining twenty-eight persons including two women and a child still aboard.

Efforts made to salvage the *Broadmayne* were unsuccessful and fortunately there was no serious oil spillage and no loss of life. She was sold to Messrs John & Co, Port Talbot, for disposal. Soon after, her stern broke away and slipped into deep water so the larger remaining portion, bow and mid-ships, was patched and on a very high tide she was floated to nearby Mill Bay Cove, adjacent to Kingswear Castle. There she was cut up for scrap iron, which was taken to Kingswear Station for dispatch by rail for smelting in South Wales. Today, at very low tide, some boilers and a few plates are still visible.

After the carnage of the recent Great War, change was inevitable but often unpalatable. There was now a surplus to requirements of ten million tons of shipping, and as a major coal bunkering port the harbour depended on the number of calling steamships. The diminished number, and the fact that most new vessels being built were now oil fired, meant that the trade slowly declined. But fortunately for the cash-starved Harbour Commission, the arrival in 1921 of the SS *Glenbridge* to lay up in the harbour was closely followed by six more; then a positive plethora of vessels came, many from the Prince Line of steamers, until the harbour was crowded with ranks of laid up steamers. This partly compensated for the loss of revenue from the declining coaling trade, but the last of the laid up vessels left in 1952. Today the harbour is equally crowded with small yachts but lacking the romantic appeal of the old steamers.

33 1923 *ST PATRIES* a steam tanker

In June 1923 an unusual occurrence in the harbour was the arrival and the sinking of the tanker SS *St. Patries*. She had been wrecked elsewhere and had been purchased by a German firm. Her bottom plates had been torn but they had raised her, and with the aid of tanks and powerful pumps were in the process of towing her to Germany for repair and return to service. Unfortunately, in bad weather off the harbour and having shipped a considerable amount of water, her pumps broke down and she showed signs of settling again. So they made for the harbour and managed to get as far as Ballast Cove before sinking again.

Engineers from Philips managed to repair the pumps and clear the tanks and hull, but doubts were expressed as to the advisability and safety of continuing the journey. It was suggested it would be safer to either repair or abandon her here. But the German owners persisted and she left for Germany.

Three weeks later, the following brief report appeared in the *Chronicle*: The bottomless vessel, SS *St Patries*, recently from this port, on her return journey in tempestuous weather to Germany, took the waters and sank four miles South West of West Hinder. This proved the wisdom of the advice the owners had thought fit to ignore and the vessel had the dignity of slipping her tow and joining Father Neptune.

Dartmouth Harbour

⑨⑨ = *site of vessel described and numbered in text*

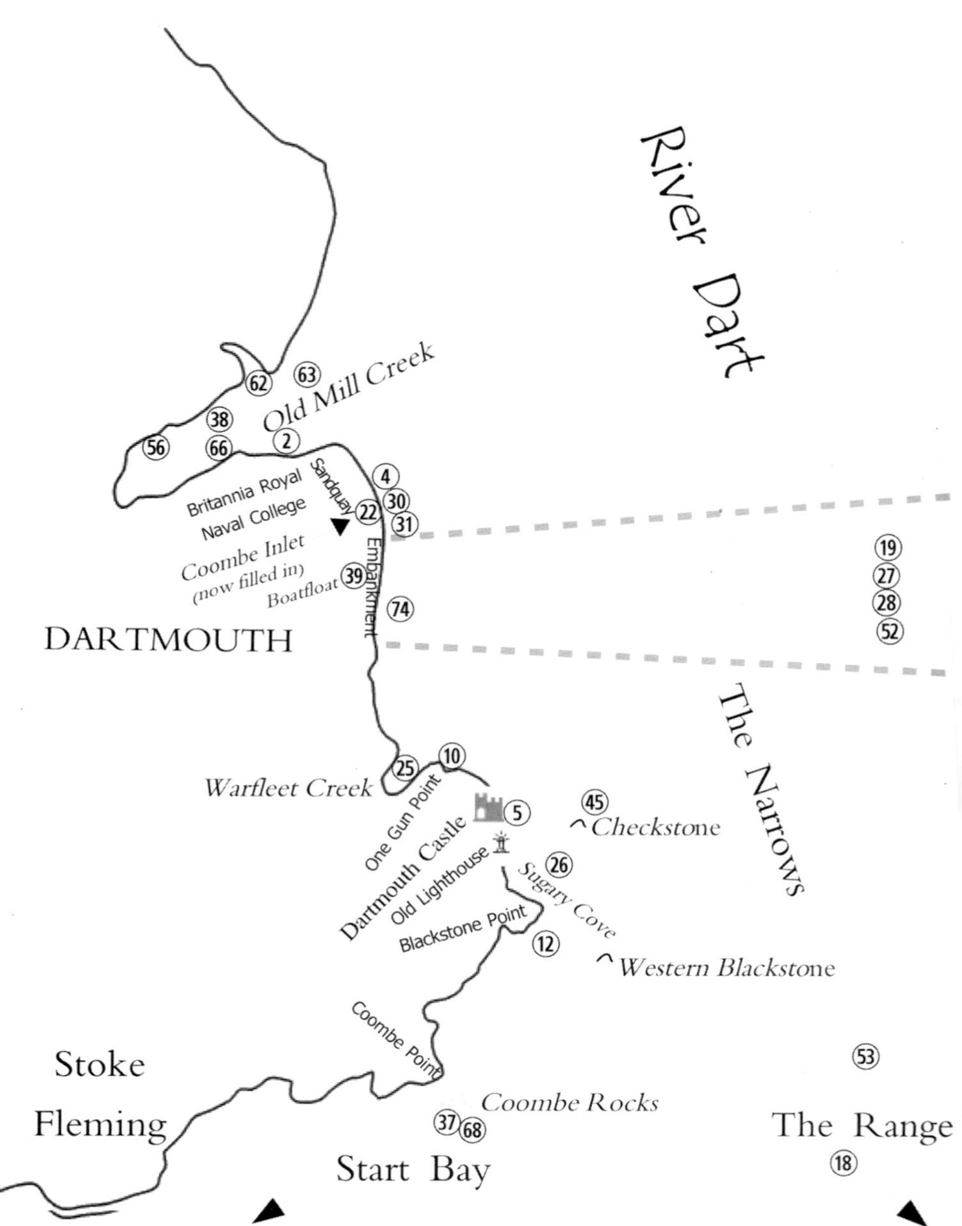

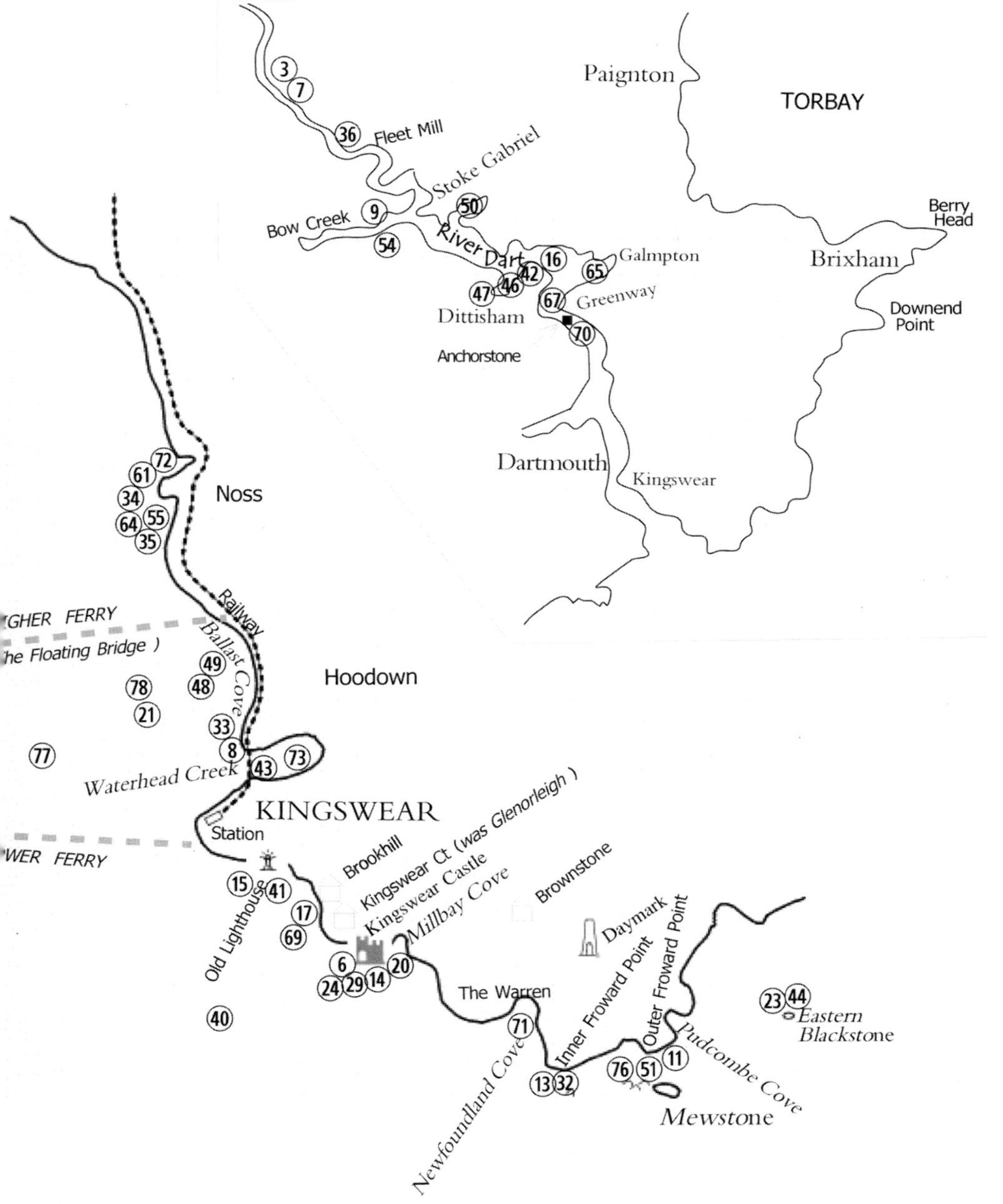

58 59 60 75
at sea elsewhere

Not to Scale
The River & creeks are widened for clarity

34 1924 *FLOATING DOCK* Philip and Sons (see also No.61, page 40)

The Floating Dock *at Sandquay, connected to the shore via the turtle back Torpedo Boat Destroyer* TBD14 *(No.64, page 42)* *Derek Blackhurst*

In the spring of 1924, Philips' North Country partners, Swan & Hunter Co Ltd, purchased a much needed asset for Dartmouth harbour.

The newly acquired *Floating Dock* 260ft ×58ft, with a capacity for 1,500tons and 14ft draft, arrived in the tow of a Dutch tug and was moored at Noss. A few days later the German full rigged barque, the *Landkirchen*, went ashore at Downend Point, and was recovered by the tug. She was berthed in the *Floating Dock* and work began, but later when the crew were settling in, the dock lurched to starboard. The forty-one members of the crew were ordered ashore, and the dock sank. Fortunately, the *Landkirchen*, free of her mooring ties, had floated out mainly trouble free from the sinking dock.

After the Falmouth salvage vessel *Ringdove Aid* had made several unsuccessful attempts to raise her, Philips finally applied to the Harbour Commission for permission for the *Floating Dock* to be left there as a permanent wreck, for with her two sides cut off she would have 30ft of clear water over her at spring tides. Permission was refused, so the salvage ship departed and the dry dock's tanks were sealed and filled with compressed air. She rose to the surface, and after repositioning at Sandquay, gave continuous service for another thirty-seven years.

35 1925 *MAYFLY* an ex-Mersey ferry

Back in 1893, Dartmouth's Port Sanitary Authority (PSA) had to comply with a Government edict that all ports and harbours were to have a remote floating isolation hospital to safeguard the general public. The PSA purchased the paddle steamer *Mayfly* 728tons, an ex-Mersey ferry built in 1863. She had saloons, promenade decks, was double plated, and was

PS Mayfly *stationed off Noss Point*

fitted out on the Dart as a hospital ship. She cost £700 of the £1,000 allowed and was permanently moored at Noss Point. After forty odd years she had deteriorated and in 1909 the authorities ordered her leaking hull to be lined with a layer of concrete and hauled closer inshore to the river bank. In later years efforts were made to acquire a replacement vessel, but funding was always insufficient. The first was the old *Britannia's* tender, HMS *Wave,* which proved too expensive as did several other Admiralty vessels the PSA inspected. They persisted and travelled the country to inspect several other potential vessels all to no avail, while the old *Mayfly* became almost untenable. A few rusting remains and the outline of her sponsons were once visible at low tide at the entrance of Old Mill Creek.

36 1925 *KINGSWEAR CASTLE I* River Dart Steamboat Co

Kingswear Castle I was a paddle steamer built in Falmouth and commissioned by Philips in 1903 and she became the RDSC's fourth paddle steamer. In 1925 after 22 years river service she was redundant; her engines were removed and fitted into the new *Kingswear Castle II.* The engineless hull was fitted out as a quarantine fever ship by the Port Sanitary Authority. After several years she was stripped, and towed up river towards Totnes where in Fleet Mill Inlet she was holed and sunk. Her remains lie there against the bank to this day.

PS Kingswear Castle I, *in her heyday off Dartmouth*
Cyril King

The resting place of Kingswear Castle I *at Fleet Mill Quay*
R Clammer

37 1926 *LORD KITCHENER* a Thames barge

In June 1926 severe gales caused the wreck and loss of two of the three crew of a London sailing barge on Coombe Rocks. The *Lord Kitchener,* a flat-bottomed Thames sailing barge, 150tons, owned by F T Everard & Sons, London, left Poole with a crew of three on 16 June for Par, Cornwall, for a load of china clay.

She came round Portland with a north east wind, but fifteen miles below the Bill the wind shifted to south east, and at midnight changed to due south and blowing a gale. She was hauled close to the wind, the topsail and mainsail were taken off to run steady with just the foresail and jib. By 4am there was heavy hail and with visibility considerably reduced land loomed ahead. The anchors were dropped, but she dragged and went broadside onto the Coombe Rocks, smashing a hole into her heads forward and breaking the stern. With water pouring in she foundered. The dinghy was smashed to pieces, so the crew climbed up the mainmast with the boy at the top, then the mate, followed by the captain. They clung there for thirty minutes until the shrouds broke and the tall mainmast fell towards the shore and into the sea. They worked their way forward hoping to make the rocks, but a huge wave swept them all into the seething waters. The mate and cabin boy were swept away and not seen again, but the captain was washed under the mast and was nearly suffocated by surrounding wreckage. A wave crashed him onto the rocks, and with great difficulty he worked his way ashore.

The time then was approximately 4.30am so he searched the shore for three hours without success looking for his companions. With difficulty he climbed the eighty foot high cliff in the dark and walked to Redlap Farm. There Mr and Mrs Timewell found him and with true Devon hospitality gave him a stimulant, hot drinks and a bath. They provided him with some clothes, and he remained with them for three weeks.

At the inquest, farmer Yardesly, Poundsgate Farm said:

'*On Sunday I visited the wreck and from the cliffs I saw a body in the sea, so I climbed down and strode into the water and pulled the body ashore. It was naked and later proved to be the mate. Nearby I saw another body which I also pulled onto the beach. It was clad only in a jersey and a boot, and was that of the boy.*'

The coastguards recovered the bodies and sent them by train from Kingswear Station for burial in their hometown of Erith, Kent. A year or so later, at the dangerous headland of Coombe Point, a watch-cabin was erected with telephone connection.

Later in 1926 the Harbour Commission expressed their concern that the coaling companies had between them abandoned five hulks which were disintegrating on Ballast Cove foreshore and ordered that the wrecks be demolished, using explosives if necessary.

38 1929 *SIX BROTHERS* a Brixham trawler

The mule class trawler *Six Brothers* built in Jackman's Brixham yard for Mr John Ellis in 1897 was registered DH441 but re-registered BM144 by his son in 1919. During 1929 she was dismantled for a hulk and eventually in 1967 run up on the North side of Old Mill Creek, where today some remains can still be seen.

39 1930 *CAM* a Kings Lynn dredger – the boat that failed to float in the Boat Float.

In 1928 in Dartmouth the long overdue scheme to extend the 1878/1885 South Embankment with a new North Embankment extension commenced. By 1930 the work was well advanced, and the *Cam*, a King's Lynn steam dredger, had completed the backpumping of silt into the old Coombe Inlet behind the new embankment. The Corporation then negotiated a four-week extension of the *Cam's* contract, to pump the years of accumulated silt in the town-centre Boat Float out into the river.

The dredger with her funnel and deck fittings lowered, was manoeuvred under the road bridge spanning the entrance to the Boat Float and moored centrally. Her discharge pipe was connected to a series of ten inch pipes laid through the Royal Avenue Gardens and along the side of the embankment road in order to discharge the silt as filling in the old Coombe Inlet, behind the new North Embankment. Work commenced and was at an advanced stage when the *Cam* suddenly developed a list to starboard and began to fill with water. The fires were extinguished to prevent explosion, and she settled under the waters of the Boat Float to become on object of humour to the town's people. Some days later she was raised and completed the task, and under tow left for Kings Lynn.

The Cam *underwater in the Boat Float with the discharge pipes on the surface* *R Tucker/Dartmouth Museum*

40 1932 *TEST* BM93 a Brixham trawler

The *Test* built in Exmouth in 1928 was in collision on 15 August 1932 with the excursion paddle steamer *Duke of Devonshire* (see No.65, page 42) and foundered to the east of the River entrance.

41 1931 *GOOD INTENT* a pilot boat

A mishap occurred in 1931 below the Lighthouse in Bakers Cove, Kingswear, to the pilot cutter *Good Intent*. Pilots R Gatzias and R H Roberts, on returning from piloting the Swedish SS *Valencia* to the pilot limits, nearly lost their lives when an explosion blew Gatzias through the engine room roof and caused the

Good Intent to burst into flames. Both men had to leap overboard, and although Roberts had a life jacket he could not swim, so Gatzias swam ashore for help. A Mr Walsh who lived at 'Inverdart' swam out to support Roberts until a boat from the nearby Kingswear house, 'Riversea', rescued the men. Meanwhile, the Dartmouth Coaling Company's launch *Meroe* arrived and towed the blazing *Good Intent* to Warfleet Creek, where they pierced a hole in her side and she sank.

Mr Walsh received an award for his gallantry.

42 1931 *IRENE* a ketch

The River Dart's quiet creeks are resting places where many vessels from the sea ended their days. Local folklore says a trader which may well have been the former schooner *Esther* built in Shaldon in 1856, was hulked after the end of the Great War and about 1931 was converted to a substantial houseboat called the *Irene.* After thefts of valuable fittings from the vessel, she was driven ashore in a gale. At low water on the south side of the entrance to Dittisham Creek opposite Blackness Rock the stark ribs of her large wooden hull can be seen. Here and in Old Mill Creek owners frequently had their vessels hauled ashore to serve as substantial houseboats for many more years.

43 1935 wooden float of the ***LOWER FERRY III***

On Whit Monday holiday 1935 a serious incident occurred on the river. This could have had far reaching consequences when the *Lower Ferry*, fortunately empty of passengers and vehicles, was struck by the Admiralty Yacht *Enchantress* while going to take up station. The deckhand aboard the ferry float had just sufficient time to scramble aboard the tug *Hauley* before the tow ropes parted, and the old wooden float sank mid-stream in deep water (see No.73, page 47). The second new metal float was pressed into service to maintain service to the flow of holiday traffic, and the Channel Coaling Co moored a small hulk with red flags and lights over the wreck. The float's remains were raised two days later and run up on the Kingswear shore and removed to Waterhead Creek.

The remains, seen here in 1991, of the old wooden float of Lower Ferry III *still lying in Waterhead Creek, Kingswear*
Harold Hutchins

44 1936 *TAUREAU* a French tug

In July 1936 disaster overtook *Taureau*, a large French tug on passage from Rotterdam to Leixous, Portugal. Having coaled at Brixham, she left near midnight in thick rain and poor visibility. At 12.30am just outside Dartmouth harbour she struck the Eastern Blackstone with some force and was to sink within minutes.

The engines were on the verge of exploding when the chief mate, one of the seven crew, was washed overboard but hung on to the anchor chain. The remaining crew, including an injured fireman still aboard, launched the ship's boat and rescued the chief mate, and surprisingly set a course for return to Brixham. They kept flashing an SOS with their Morse lamp, which was observed by the Brixham trawler *Owl* (one of Brixham's first six steam trawlers), which picked them up and proceeded to Brixham. They were admitted to hospital where the fireman died.

45 1937 SS *ENGLISH TRADER* a grain carrier

RNLI Bronze Clasp Wm HH MOGRIDGE

SS English Trader*, bow on the Checkstone after separation.* *R Tucker/Dartmouth Museum*

The *English Trader* had been built in 1934 at Furness as the *Arctees* and was carrying a cargo of grain from the Argentine. On 23 January the *English Trader*, 362ft long, when calling for bunkers, sailed too close to Dartmouth Castle, and ran hard on to the Checkstone Ledge lodging solid. The wind increased to a gale from the SSE and the heavy swell lifted the *English Trader*, swung her stern round and was pounding her bows heavily on the rocks. Seas 15feet high were breaking over the steamer and the captain thought she could last no longer. The lifeboat which had stood by all night closed at once. The position of the fifty-two men on board was extremely hazardous.

SS English Trader *being towed stern-first on her way to South Shields for repair, passes her bow section off the Checkstone*

R Tucker/Dartmouth Museum

For weeks the town's inhabitants daily turned out to watch developments.

The combined efforts over several days of the destroyer HMS *Witch* and four tugs failed to free her. On the thirteenth day her forward tanks became holed and her bows broke away just aft of her foremast. Ship surgery became urgent so heavy timber bulkheads were erected by divers and powerful pumps cleared water from the main body of the ship. The damaged fore section was cut away from the main hull. Now floating free, the main body was towed stern first into the harbour and beached at Ballast Cove, Kingswear. There the temporary bulkheads were reinforced and braced with steel hawsers. She was then towed stern first to South Shields where a new forward section was built, and one hundred days after going aground the *English Trader* returned to service! Meanwhile the abandoned bow section was cut up, loaded into barges and taken to Kingswear where it was dumped on the foreshore for onward transmission by rail to South Wales for scrap.

The reconstructed *English Trader* survived until 1941 when she was finally wrecked on the Hammond Knoll off the East coast.

46 1937 *FIERY CROSS* a trawler and two companions

Headline gripping wrecks like the *English Trader* dominated both national and local news, yet the barely reported demise of much loved and sometimes ungainly vessels can bring similar grief to the owners. Such must have been the case for the 1905 Porthleven-built *Fiery Cross* whose derelict remains – keel, sternpost, and rudder – lie at the head of Dittisham Creek. Until World War I she fished off the east coast, later transferring to Brixham registering as BM145, and until 1933 her home waters were the English Channel. She was sold away and used as a houseboat until 1937, then abandoned, deteriorating and stripped of timbers, she survived until the end of World War II.

47 1937 *SHORTEST DAY* a Plymouth ketch

Along the shore from *Fiery Cross* are the remains of *Shortest Day*, a 75ton ketch rigged barge which carried grain or stone cargoes from Plymouth to Falmouth. She was teak on steel and was hulked for the Dart coaling trade before being stripped of her valuable timber in Dittisham Creek.

48 1937 Floating Crane Grabs

Also in 1937, not one, but two of the coaling companies' old 1917 floating coal grabs sank in a gale, probably through old age and lack of maintenance. They presented an unusual picture with just their masts and jibs showing above the water. They were raised, run up on Ballast Cove foreshore and demolished where they lay. Later, a new larger up-to-date floating crane replaced the two old floating grabs.

Floating Crane *sunk at Ballast Cove, Kingswear*

49 1937 a coaling hulk

Near the *Fiery Cross* and the *Shortest Day* in Dittisham Creek are the remains of an old teak-on-steel coaling hulk, which when condemned, was bought for her timbers which could be used in the antique trade.

50 1938 *GLORY* BM16 a Brixham trawler

On the north foreshore of Stoke Gabriel creek there are the remains of the 35ton Brixham trawler *Glory*. She was built in 1906 by Sanders of Galmpton for owner/skipper Mr Ellis and she was a several times winner of the King George V cup at the annual Brixham Trawler Race. In 1929 she was sold for use as a houseboat, but two owners later broke loose from her moorings sustaining hull damage. In 1938 she was declared unsafe, run up on the hard, and is now baptised by the incoming tides twice daily.

The bones of Glory *on the beach at Stoke Gabriel* *Martin Langley / Edwina Small*

51 1937 *WHITE LADY* a Torquay pleasure steamer

The *Chronicle* reported on 23 June an embarrassment that could have developed into a major disaster.

White Lady *aground off the Mewstone* *Gordon Thomas*

The pleasure steamer *White Lady* with 74 passengers on board was on passage from Torquay to the River Dart. The shipmaster decided to take the shorter inshore route past the dangerous Mewstone, and with some force struck fast on the reef. Much to the passengers' alarm she developed a 30 degree list to starboard. Fortunately the weather remained fine and her predicament was seen by other cruising boats and yachts. With the aid of dinghies, the passengers were transferred and landed at Kingswear for a return journey by train to Torquay.

As the hull was not holed, she was later freed on a full tide and with the aid of Philips yard-boats, taken to their Noss Works.

This near disaster had close local Kingswear connections, for back in 1925 the GWR decided to dispose of their Lower Ferry Service, and their chairman, Sir Felix Pole, gave the floats, landing slips and Waterhead Creek to Dartmouth Corporation for a nominal £25. In 1926 the Corporation decided to put the ferry service out to tender, but received only two replies. One, to show his disgust, was a blank offer from the former operator, Tom Casey. His family for nearly fifty years—since 1877—had run the service. Since its closure he had for a short ten months, with his small twelve-seat launch *I'll Try*, started to run a private service to Dartmouth from Longford Steps, adjacent to the Lower Ferry Slip.

The other quotation was from Kingswear based W J Peters, now owner of the *White Lady*, together with a Mrs Heseltine. This tender was successful and it was Mr Peters who, under contract, ran the service for the Corporation. During his ten years he acquired from boatbuilder Peter Mitchell of Portmellon, the first three of the eventual total of seven numbered *Hauley* ferry float tugs. In 1936 his interest moved to creating a quality holiday steamboat service from Torquay to the Dart, so with the Corporation's permission, he surrendered his lease to the General Estates Company Ltd who thereafter ran the service. Shortly after the end of World War II, the Company decided not to seek renewal of the lease and subsequently Dartmouth Corporation and South Hams District Council took over the running of the service as they do today.

At that time changes in the harbour were becoming obvious, for the numbers of coal fired ships calling for bunkers – the port's staple industry for eighty-five years – had been steadily declining, and any new vessels being built were predominantly oil fired. Meanwhile, the actions of the Third Reich were casting long shadows over Europe, and the 'dogs of war' were stirring. On 3 September 1939, near twenty years since the end of the Great War, there came the Second World War. Preparations for war proceeded afoot, and the laid up shipping above Noss – the 'graveyard', as the locals called it – was rapidly mobilised as all redundant shipping was called into service; the coal trade was reprieved until its final demise in 1952.

52 1942 *FERNWOOD* and ***DAGNY*** coaling hulks in the German air-raids

In 1942 the harbour was full of warships but remained clear of conflict until 11am on 18 September 1942, when the harbour suffered its first air raid. Against the morning sun, six Fokker Wolf fighter-bombers flew down the river and paired off to attack the college, coaling installations and the shipyard. The college was machine gunned, hit and damaged by two bombs which caused the death of a Wren officer. Two more attacked the Philips shipyards at Noss, causing considerable damage and leaving twenty men dead and forty injured.

The remaining pair concentrated on the *Fernwood* which along with the *Witch* and *Dagny* were coal storage hulks and moored permanently in midstream.

The collier *Fernwood*, 2,555tons, a steel screw steamer built in 1923 was sunk with 700tons of coal on board. Fortunately there was no loss of life, and the collier was later raised, repaired and returned to service.

The coaling hulk *Dagny* was also sunk, and sadly four men were lost, but later this large hulk was raised and returned to service.

Dagny, *a large but typical standing coaling hulk permanently moored mid-river. She was formerly a full rigged clipper ship*

John Horsley/Brixham Museum

A crane grab stationed alongside the *Dagny* also sank but with no loss of life, and later was recovered and returned to service. Several men were rescued from the water by a brave Wren in a tender for which she was later rewarded for her courage by the owners of the Coaling Company.

On 13 February 1943, the town centre was the subject of a further and sustained vicious aerial attack that caused several casualties and considerable damage in Duke Street and Foss Street and in particularly to the town's historic Butterwalk. This was the last aerial attack on the town.

53 1942 *ISÈRE* a Free French tug and the loss of a J class yacht

While being towed by a trawler from Brixham to Fowey, a large J-Class yacht with only a Brixham deckhand Thomas Bray on board encountered furious storms when only eleven miles out; this made the yacht unmanageable. They turned to seek the shelter of Dartmouth harbour, but in the entrance the tow parted; the trawler managed to pull alongside and another rope was thrown to Mr Bray who secured it to the towing post. Unfortunately the post broke. With great difficulty another rope was hurled aboard, and this was secured to the winch, but this also broke away. By now things were critical and their plight was seen by Captain Leon F Coquerel, commander of the Dartmouth-based Free French Force's tug *Isère* who steamed out and succeeded in drawing close enough for two of his crew members to scramble on board the yacht.

Captain Coquerel on Isère

Reg and Sheila Little

By now the seas were mountainous and they were unable to reach Mr Bray, who sadly was washed overboard from the stern and drowned. The yacht quickly began to sink so the two *Isère* crewmen jumped overboard, one managing to swim to the safety of the tug but the other, when some twenty yards away, began to drown. Captain Coquerel bravely jumped overboard into the raging sea, and with great difficulty secured the man until a launch arrived and hauled Captain Coquerel and the unconscious seaman aboard.

The town and the council were so impressed by this act of 'entente-cordiale gallantry' that the Mayor awarded to Captain Coquerel the Royal Humane Society bronze medal, bar, and certificate, at a civic gathering in the Guildhall.

In 1945 the war ended and the men – some of them – returned and normality was slowly regained. The port quickly filled with decommissioned British and foreign warships, which were gradually dispersed.

54 1945 Two of the **Belgian trawler fleet**

When hostilities started, there were eight Belgian wooden trawlers fishing out of Brixham but all were interned in the Dart for the duration of the war. Some were used as service vessels in the river during the war but in 1945 six were returned to Belgium. Two had so deteriorated that they were condemned and left ashore in the Dart on the south side of the entrance to Bow Creek where their remains lie today, washed by every tide.

The two remaining trawlers at the entrance to Bow Creek *Martin Langley/Edwina Small*

55 1945 *CAPORAL PEUGOT* a French steam trawler

Caporal Peugot *in Noss Creek*

A French wooden steam trawler, believed to be the *Caporal Peugot*, was beached on the river bank at Noss. She had served as a minesweeper for the French government and had assisted in the evacuation of French and British troops out of Dunkirk and Cherbourg. After the fall of France, and with engine damage, she was taken under tow to Plymouth where she was impounded by the Royal Navy and then later moved for service on the Dart. By 1945 her condition had badly deteriorated, and so permission was sought from Philips shipbuilders that she could be run up and abandoned in Lower Noss Creek to help retain the mud; her bones can still be seen.

56 1947 *DARTMOUTH CASTLE II* a paddle steamer

The *Dartmouth Castle II* had so deteriorated that she was abandoned where she lay at Creekside Boatyard, Old Mill Creek, and serves as a retaining wall and wharf extension. Today the skeleton of her hull and sponsons can still be seen (see picture page 14)

57 1923-1967 *TOTNES CASTLE* a paddle steamer

PS Totnes Castle II (Mayfly *in the background) in the River Dart*

The *Totnes Castle II* failed her inspection in 1963, and in 1967 broke her tow on the way to the Plymouth breaker's yard, and had the dignity of sinking at sea.

58 1947 *WESTWARD* a J-class yacht

This superb yacht with a long and colourful history, was designed and built by Herreshof at Bristol, Rhode Island, USA in 1910 for an American, Alexander S Cochrane. After crossing the Atlantic in fourteen days, at the Kiel Regatta of 1910 she handily won the Emperor's Cup in a four-race series during which Kaiser Wilhelm II's *Meteor IV* suffered a broken bowsprit in a collision with *Westward*. Her performance so impressed the Germans that she was bought by a German company, and renamed *Hamburg II*. In 1913, the Kaiser attended the Dartmouth Regatta in *Meteor V*, mooring in the harbour alongside and later racing against King George V who was in his J Class yacht *Britannia*.

In 1914 *Hamburg II* (ex *Westward*) was seized in Cowes by the British at the outbreak of World War I. In 1923 re-named *Westward*, she was purchased by Thomas Benjamin Davis, a native of the Channel Islands. Under Davis in 1935, *Westward* beat every other vessel in the Royal Yacht Squadron's Regatta. He attended all the Dartmouth regattas in her, competing against all the famous J Class yachts *Astra, Britannia, Candida, Endeavour, Shamrock V, Velsheda* and *Yankee.* After the death of Mr Davies and in accordance with his will, just before the 1947 regatta she was stripped down in preparation for her sinking. She was lashed to the Dartmouth tug *Portwey* and under the command of harbourmaster Captain Griffiths and with sirens blowing, she left her beloved River Dart for the last time to be blown up in the Hurd Deep, off Jersey, Mr Davis's home and where he had based *Westward* for many years.

Westward *lashed alongside* Portwey *on her way to scuttling.* *Dave Griffiths*

During 1951 there was a brief revival in the port, when the gas-coal trade was renewed by F T Everards & Sons Ltd, with a line of handsome coasters, *Similarity, Serenity, Security,* and other like named vessels (several local men, Dave Griffiths, Eddie Smales etc today remember serving aboard). The coal was unloaded over Kingswear's Quays for delivery by rail to the Torquay Hollicombe Gas Works; it ceased in 1963. Then there were coasters carrying timber to Totnes until the early eighties, after which all commercial traffic on the river ceased.

59 1951 *AMARYLLIS* a Naval College yacht

This 37ton yawl *Amaryllis* had a rich and colourful history, for in 1920 she belonged to Lt G H P Mulhauser, who in three years single-handedly circumnavigated the globe in a voyage of 31,159 miles from Dartmouth to Dartmouth. When he died in 1924 she was presented to the College by his sister as a training craft on the understanding that

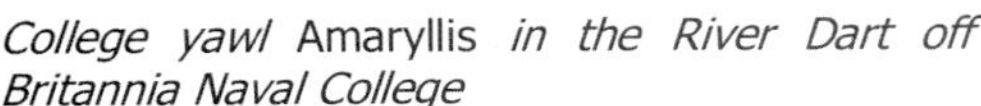

College yawl Amaryllis *in the River Dart off Britannia Naval College*

when her days were over she was to be sunk at sea. In 1935 the yawl showed her preference for the Dart as a last resting place, when she suffered an explosion which seriously injured her caretaker/skipper; only the prompt action of the College saved her. She survived and in 1951 a convoy of College boats accompanied her to Start Point where she was blown apart, joining the sea nymphs below.

60 1952 ***SORKNESS*** a standing hulk

In 1952, as the number of coal burning ships remaining in commission was negligible and all new vessels being now oil fired, the last rites were read for the port's one hundred year bunkering trade. The small shifting hulks were beached and broken up, while the three main standing hulks, the *Juno, Sorkness,* and the *Dagny* were towed away for breaking up elsewhere; the *Sorkness* had the dignity of breaking her tow and sinking at sea! A strange quiet descended on the harbour until a depression in seafaring trade brought some surplus shipping back to lie up for a few years in the river above Noss.

Standing hulk Sorkness, *with tug alongside, off Kingswear* *Dave Griffiths*

61 1956 ***FLOATING DOCK*** containing MV ***SEYYID KHALIFA***

Seyyid Khalifa *in the collapsed* Floating Dock
Roy Jones

On 5 February, when *Seyyid Khalifa* was nearing completion in Philips yard, the dock began to fill with water because of a corroded manhole cover, and the crew were immediately ordered ashore. As the dock sank, the vessel began to heel over, and slipped off her keel blocks, but on the following day on a rising tide the vessel floated free, and continued on her voyage. At low water, with the aid of the Harbour Authority the dock was pumped out, raised and repaired. It was inspected by Lt Commander Collinson RN, for the Admiralty, who downgraded the Dock to a 500ton capacity, which made its functioning un-economic. So in 1960, it was replaced by a slipway cradle and winding gear. With the loss of the commercial shipping, trade for the port's only remaining shipyard Philips & Son declined, and by 1961 it was decided that their *Floating Dock* was no longer required, so in May the tug *Meeching* arrived to tow her up north for scrapping.

This unfortunate event also made the two connection gantries and the central former supporting destroyer hulk *TBD14* redundant; the latter was abandoned nearby, as recorded below (No.64, see page 42).

62 late 1950s *WINIFRED* a ketch

She was built in Falmouth in 1897 and registered 38tons. Out of some sixty years, she was thirty years in service from Plymouth to Portsmouth and Fareham. She survived two world wars, and in the second served the Admiralty, delivering supplies to the barrage balloon ships in Falmouth harbour. Her last years when not doing service for the river's American forces were spent trading from Brixham harbour. Her remains lie in a small inlet on the north side of Old Mill Creek.

63 1965 *INVERMORE* a schooner

She lies on the north side of the mouth of Old Mill Creek on Rough Point flats. She was built in 1921 at Arklow, as a 146ton three-masted schooner for general trade, in which she was one of the last to serve. She was sold away in 1956 and later bought by a group of misguided enthusiasts who dreamed of taking paying emigrants to Australia. In 1960 they arrived, cash-starved, in Dartmouth harbour, where she was abandoned. Five years later with harbour dues unpaid, she was towed to her present position and left to the mercy of wind and tide, which have taken their toll. Today little remains other than a few gaunt timbers; her Widdop two cylinder engine is now

The schooner Invermore *abandoned on Rough Point flats, Old Mill Creek* *Dave Griffiths*

in the National Maritime Museum. In the 1960s two well known local men, Chris Ruddlestone and the late Chris Bircham, fitted some of her timbers into the bar of the former Gunfield Hotel, regrettably a hotel no longer.

64 ***TBD 14*** a torpedo-boat destroyer

For thirty-seven years the *Floating Dock* had been connected to the shore at Sandquay by a bridge of two single span bowed girder gantries supported centrally by the stripped down buoyant hulk of the *TBD14*, which had been purchased from the Admiralty. *TBD14* was an early turtle decked destroyer, circa 1898, the last period of these destroyers. This bridge became surplus to requirements so the girder bridges were dismantled and the destroyer's hull was towed across the river to Lower Noss Creek adjacent to their Noss Works, and run aground, being left to disintegrate alongside the remains of the abandoned French trawler, the *Caporal Peugot* (No.55, page 37).

65 1968 ***DUKE OF DEVONSHIRE*** a sea-going paddle steamer

PS Duke of Devonshire*; passengers embarking at Blackpool Sands*

This 257ton, 175ft long regular Dartmouth visitor was built in 1896 by R&H Green in London. She was designed to run up on the beach to load/unload passengers. She spent decades visiting Dartmouth and south coast resorts with her sister, the *Duchess of Devonshire.*

She was exceptional in that during World War I she was converted for minesweeping and steamed to the Middle East to serve in the Gallipoli campaign, then later passed through the Suez Canal to partake in actions in the Persian Gulf. She then returned to her quiet pastoral Devonshire coastal service. In 1936 she was acquired by Cosens & Co who renamed her *Consul*, and she continued her South Devon coastal tours which included Dartmouth. By 1963 the service had become unprofitable so she was offered for sale.

PS Duke of Devonshire *derelict at Galmpton before scrapping in Southampton..*

She was purchased by Peter Blyth, an orthodontist from Clevedon, Somerset, for his Sail-a-Boat Holidays. She was moored below the Higher Ferry as a dinghy sailing centre but in 1968 was sold for breaking up at Southampton.

Two hulks converted to houseboats in Galmpton Creek.

These were the sunset years for the busy centuries old coastal trade, carried out by the small sailing and steam vessels which had served our coastlines; today there are only a few survivors. Wrecks by storm and mishap fortunately were becoming a rarity but many of the old vessels survived to seek solace in the quiet backwaters of the River Dart, some to end their days as wrecks or houseboats.

66 Post WWII *MIZPAH* a sand dredging ketch

Her final resting place lies on the southern shoreline of Old Mill Creek, in the shadow of Sir Henry Paul Seale's once castellated stone built estate folly. She was a 54ton ketch, built in 1898 at Kingsbridge by William Date for general trading by Plymouth owners. Later she was acquired by the Langmead family of Galmpton, who had just secured the contract to supply River Dart sand and gravel for the construction of Torquay's new Haldon Pier.

Mizpah *at rest Old Mill Creek*

Martin Langley

For the contract, along with a partner ketch *Effort,* she was fitted with an auxiliary engine. Later the Langmeads purchased a sizeable steam vessel equipped with the latest dredging equipment, which rendered the two ketches superfluous. It is thought that both also served as barrage balloon ships on the Dart. Finally the *Mizpah* was run up in this corner of Arcadia, and also made a contribution to nautical memorabilia, as her pump windlass is incorporated in a foredeck display in the National Maritime Museum.

67 post WWII *EFFORT* a ketch

She was also built by William Date, Kingsbridge shipbuilder, early in the 1880's, possibly for Salcombe owners for general coastal trading. Then she was acquired by the Galmpton Langmead family carrying sand and gravel for their Torquay Haldon Pier contract, and as stated above she became redundant when they acquired a modern dredging unit. Later she did service as a barrage balloon vessel on the Dart and suffered damage from a near miss. It is widely thought that the sizeable vandalised ship's timbers near Greenway Quay, are those of the ketch *Effort,* two miles upstream of her workmate *Mizpah.*

Langmead's ketches Mizpah *and* Effort *in Torquay harbour*

68 c:1960 Capt Cooke's (lady skipper) **MFV,**

She was a naval reserve/auxiliary services ship on passage from Portland in dense fog under skilful dead reckoning. There was no bell on the Castle Ledge buoy and in the poor visibility she overran and struck Coombe Rocks. She was holed but towed into the Dart and settled off Lower Noss Point opposite the Naval College. She was later pumped out and taken under tow heading for Southampton but crossing Lyme Bay she continued taking water and was returned to the Dart. She was put on the Admiralty sales list, sold and towed away by her new owner.

MFV settled on the mud Lower Noss Point *John Distin*

69 c1970 *SPANKER* a coaster in ballast

After unloading in the river, she was passing between the castles in a strong south westerly wind and being high in the water with her propeller cavitating she went aground on the rocks on the eastern side but quickly managed to get off again.

Spanker *temporarily on the rocks near Kingswear Castle*
Dave Griffiths

70 1971 ***ESTHER COLEEN*** **PZ232** a Brixham trawler.

Esther Coleen *a Brixham trawler 'safely' on the Anchorstone*

Dave Griffiths

With the owner, not the skipper, in charge she was trying below Dittisham to avoid a timber ship coming down river, and in doing so ran aground on the Anchorstone. Fortune smiled and she came to rest leaning dramatically against the pole but suffered no damage and was refloated on a following tide.

71 1972 ***DOROTHEA*** a crabber

The *Dorothea* put to sea on a very rough night in February 1972, when all other crabbers remained on their moorings. She was an ex double ended lifeboat to which an engine had been added and it was thought her loss was caused by the fact that if she travelled at speed in such rough conditions she could easily ship water over her stern. This crabber was lost when she went ashore in Newfoundland Cove with the loss of all three of her crew, two men and a woman. The men's bodies were never recovered but the lady was found many weeks later at Thurlestone. She was identified by the fact that she had one leg longer than the other. The crabber had been owned by a Dartmouth man who was not on board at the time.

72 1981 *WESTON* a coaster

This nearly new ship under the command of a new skipper was being turned just off Philips yard prior to leaving the river. She was easing ahead towards the eastern shore but on changing to astern the gearbox failed and she gently went onto the mud. She was pulled off on a later tide and returned to the Philips yard for engine repairs.

The Weston *on the mud at Noss Point*
Dave Griffiths

73 1985 *HAULEY III* the Lower Car Ferry tug

The *Hauley III*, laid up for some time in Waterhead Creek, was one of the seven Dart tugs named Hauley. The first in 1877 was owned by the River Dart Steam Boat Co, the second in 1909 by Tom Casey, then in 1931 the present numbered line of Hauley tugs started as *Hauley I* to today's *Hauley VI* and *VII*. The *Hauley III* was built in 1932 for the Kingswear ferry crossing by Peter Mitchell, Portmellon, for Peters & Heseltine. In 1935 the *Hauley III* survived a near collision mishap in which the attached wooden ferry float sank (see No.43, page 31), was raised, and then

Hauley III *in 1985 laid up in Waterhead Creek. Owned by David Murphy but broken up due to poor condition.*

abandoned in Kingswear's Waterhead Creek. The *Hauley III* continued in service under owners General Estates and then Dartmouth Corporation until 1970. She was sold to John Distin for harbour duties. In 1985, after over fifty years service, she was purchased by an extrovert and well-liked Kingswear character, David Murphy, who hoped to use her for a book and short television series similar to the 'puffer' *Vital Spark* in the *Para Handy Tales.* Sadly her survey revealed extensive and expensive repairs were necessary, which made these plans uneconomic. So she was abandoned, and time and tide took their toll, until reluctantly, with bar and chain saw he dismembered and fired her remains where she lay in Waterhead Creek.

74 1987 *GOLDEN HIND* a replica of Drake's ship

The modern wrecking of the replica of Sir Francis Drake's famous galleon of 1577 makes an interesting and semi-romantic story.

Built in 1940 as a fishing vessel, she served in WWII and was then laid up in Rosyth. In 1950 she was converted to a replica of the 18C HMS *Centurion.* Bought in 1961 by John Reed, he converted her to the *Golden Hind* for television use as a replica of Sir Francis Drake's famous flagship and stationed her in Brixham harbour for the holiday trade.

A decade later a refit became necessary, so he engaged Arthur Curnow, coxswain of the Brixham lifeboat and owner of the local tug *Pendragon* to tow her to Philips Noss Works for a £20,000 refit, including a new keel. Because of the keel problem Arthur Curnow sensibly ran the towing warp around the whole body of the ship to equalise the strains when towing. 1988 was the four hundredth anniversary of the defeat of the Spanish Armada, and the BBC had hired a support vessel under Andrew Boyson to accompany the *Golden Hind* and take film footage for a documentary series entitled *The Armada*, and thus he was on hand to record the several stages of her sinking.

The tow commenced on Monday 9 November 1987 in reasonable weather which rapidly deteriorated and she started to take water through the shrunken planking above the waterline. Her two reconditioned pumps unfortunately failed, as did the pump on BBC's support vessel. Soon, when just off the Mewstone's rocky outcrop outside Dartmouth harbour, the only course left was to cut the tow. Mr. Boyson's boat pulled alongside the awash and sinking *Golden Hind* and John Reed with his seven crew members were taken off and transferred to *Pendragon*, now freed of her charge. The sinking was filmed from the support vessel before they and *Pendragon* returned to Brixham.

The weather improved on the third day and the tug *Pendragon* with a salvage vessel returned to search for the *Golden Hind.* They located her between Coombe Point and the Western Blackstone rock, having been carried by strong currents and tides a mile across the harbour mouth. Her topmasts were just visible above the water. There, with the aid of buoyancy air-bags she was slowly raised, exposing the fact that she had suffered some damage; her bowsprit was broken, and her fore-topmasts were missing, as was her stern walkway. Thereupon, Arthur Curnow's *Pendragon* towed her with some difficulty into Dartmouth harbour. He had hoped to moor her at Noss, near Philips shipyard, but the Harbour Authority decreed she should be moored on the South Embankment, below their offices. There, the *Golden Hind* became a source of local interest and entertainment particularly to the visitors. Supported by the buoyancy air-bags, she rose and settled – sometimes badly – with each tide, so much so that her main mast broke from the keel into two halves, the topmast falling towards the river, and the lower to the embankment.

Meanwhile, negotiations relating to insurance claims, hire charges, salvage

Golden Hind *replica supported by buoyancy bags off Dartmouth Embankment.*

costs, towage fees, harbour charges etc continued, and the Harbour Authority wanted her removed. So a national firm of salvage specialists, EuroSalve of Folkestone, was enlisted, and brought their large salvage vessel with a large bow jib crane. For the owner John Reed, mounting costs made restoration prohibitive, so he decided to write the vessel off and start again. However, the salvage company felt the vessel still had prospects, and with another partner acquired the stricken *Golden Hind* for restoration as a tourist attraction, probably in Kent near their headquarters.

Two months later an unsuccessful attempt was made to raise her by crane, and site her on a pontoon in mid-river prior to towing her to Kent, but further damage was done to her and the embankment. However, a second attempt succeeded and she was moored midstream between two fixed buoys. Shortly, she left under tow, but nothing further was ever heard of any other *Golden Hind* on display elsewhere.

Fortunately John Reed and his son located in Plymouth a former ammunition barge with a steel hull of the correct dimensions, 72ft long by 18ft wide with the correct draught. Converted, and today in Brixham harbour, numerous tourists enjoy the quality replica *Golden Hind Two.*

75 2000 *TEAM PHILIPS* a revolutionary catamaran

Leaving the Dart on trials, Team Philips *passes between the castles* *Gordon Thomas*

This review concerns mainly shipwrecks and similar disasters which have taken place in the Dart river and estuary. It seems appropriate however, to include an enormous catamaran with a revolutionary design, built on the Dart by Pete Goss at Totnes, and who in her short life generated huge local enthusiasm and attracted headlines throughout the world.

She was the twin hulled *Team Philips,* built largely of carbon fibre and with twin rotating masts, one on each hull. Her length was 120ft, width 70ft and height 138ft. The cost of £4million was funded largely by thousands of individual donors, many of whom signed their names on her hulls. It was planned for her to compete in 'The Race', a round the world speed race starting from Barcelona in December 2000. In March after leaving Dartmouth amid cheering crowds and when 35 miles off the Scilly Isles, 40ft of her port bow broke off due to a fatigue fracture. She was towed back to Totnes to rectify what proved to be a design fault. On further trials in October five months later, problems developed with her masts due to the immense pressures applied to the tiny load bearing areas.

At last in December 2000 she left the Dart to sail the 2,500 mile qualification for entering The Race. But in a fierce storm in the Atlantic, cracks developed in the central crew pod and she began to take water so badly that a Mayday distress call was sent out. This was received by the German Steamer *Hoechst Express* which rescued the seven men on board and later landed them in Nova Scotia. But the catamaran was abandoned to the sea. So ended the dreams and hopes of *Team Philips,* built to be the biggest, fastest and most high tech of boats. Its spirit lives on in a dedicated exhibition in the National Maritime Museum in Falmouth, Cornwall.

76 2002 *PRIDE OF THE DART* a passenger vessel.

Pride of the Dart *beached and flooded on Kingswear's Lighthouse Beach*
Gordon Thomas

She was originally built as a wartime local defence patrol motor launch, and was converted to a passenger vessel in 1948. On 28 June 2002 she was on an excursion passage from Torquay to Dartmouth with 26 passengers, the skipper and one crewman. Hoping to see the seals basking on the Mewstone rocks she took the inshore passage but owing to steering problems she grounded on the reef.

She was taking water fast and with manipulation of the two engines she reached the area of Dartmouth Castle where the passengers were disembarked onto the *Dart Explorer* and the *Castle Ferry*. There she lost engine power and was assisted by the harbour authority's boat to beach on Kingswear's Lighthouse Beach where she flooded. An anti-pollution boom was deployed and the next day she was made watertight and taken to a Galmpton boatyard. She was not repaired and did not sail again

77 2005 *REBEL* an ocean going ketch

In September 2005 an advertisement appeared in the Torquay based *Herald Express* reading '*Ocean going 35(sic)ft sail boat. Fibre glass. All the extras. Make a nice river side home. Owner must sell quickly. Hence £40,000. Any quick cash offer seriously considered.*' An estranged wife had put the £100,000 53ft yacht which she owned with her husband up for sale at the knockdown price of £40,000.

53ft ketch Rebel *scuttled on her mooring in Dartmouth Harbour*

That night while his wife was ashore, the enraged husband went out to the yacht and allegedly used an axe to scuttle her, smashing open seacocks below the waterline causing her to sink in the middle of Dartmouth harbour. Only the tops of her masts showed above the surface.

This unusual event caused considerable national and local interest, and also alarm in the Dart Harbour office. The frigate HMS *Sutherland* was due to moor centrally in the river to attend and support a Royal Britannia Naval College ceremony to be attended by Prince Michael of Kent. So all the stops were pulled out, and at an estimated cost of £10,000 to the already troubled owners she was raised four days later and craned ashore at a local shipyard.

78 2005 *FLOATING BRIDGE VII*

Floating Bridge VII *runs amok in the yacht moorings*

It is coincidental that our account of nautical disasters should end almost as it began. In 1855 the *Chronicle,* then in its infancy, reported the loss of *Floating Bridge No I.* Now, one hundred and fifty years later, in March 2005 the same fate nearly befell *Floating Bridge No VII.* When loaded with thirteen vehicles, she broke free of her holding cables and drifted down-river. But her bid for freedom was thwarted when she collided not with coaling steamships, as in 1855, but a grove of moored yachts. She was recovered undamaged, but it was the following day before the vehicles aboard could be unloaded and returned to their owners allowing normal ferrying service to be resumed.

THE PRESENT DAY.

There are many more than the seventy-eight wrecks in the estuary of the Dart valley recorded here, yet even in this small area they are just a tiny fraction of the keels, ribs, stern-posts, etc, just visible at low water, of dozens of other unrecorded servants of mankind, whose work done, are forgotten and lost away Also spare a thought for those hundreds of ships and their gallant crews which sailed out past the two castles, and now lie in far corners of the world, forgotten and unmourned, never to return to the Elysian green banks of the River Dart.

ACKNOWLEDGEMENTS

Once again I offer my thanks to my colleagues Neil Baxter, David Evans and Paul Moynagh for their support in collating my endeavours to formulate this third booklet.

My thanks are also due to the following for the use of information and supporting pictures (credited where known), the latter bringing life and sparkle to the text, and conveying the reader from the armchair into the field of action (without the risks).

In particular I thank Gordon Thomas, ace photographer who is as usual to the fore, as also the harbour doyen Captain Dave Griffiths, who along with the following care deeply for our corner of Arcadia:- John Behenna, Mandy Brooks, Richard Clammer, Gladys Frith, Harold Hutchings, Alan Kitteridge, Reg Little, David Murphy, John Risdon, Chris Ryan, Edwina Small, and the late Martin Langley, John Horsley, Derek Blackhurst, Rodney Tucker and R Tully.

Credit is also due to the following for the research material without which there would be no story. Firstly permission from Sir Ray Tindle owner, and Mike Roberts managing director of the South Hams Newspapers, to use material collated over the last one hundred and fifty years of publication in the weekly *Dartmouth Chronicle*. I have used also pictures from the Dartmouth Museum, Brixham Museum, *London Illustrated News*, *Yachting World*, and the Paddle Steamer Preservation Society's magazine *Paddle Wheels.* Sources are acknowledged where possible.

BIBLIOGRAPHY

The *Dartmouth Chronicle* Newspapers – 1854 to now.

Dartmouth, Percy Russell - 1950.

Bristol Channel Paddle Steamers, Robert Wall - 1973.

West Country Shipwrecks, John Behenna - 1974.

Paddle Steamers of the River Dart & Kingsbridge Estuary, Alan Kitteridge & Richard Clammer - 1980.

Lost Ships of the West Country, Martin Langley and Edwina Small - 1988.

Dartmouth and its Neighbours, Ray Freeman – 1990, revised 2007.

The Chronicles of Dartmouth, Don Collinson – 2000, revised 2002 and 2009.

Philip and Sons, Shipbuilders and Engineers, Derek Blackhurst – 2001.

Other publications by Kingswear Historians include:

The Dart Estuary Lights, Marks & Lighthouses by Don Collinson 2004

A Short History of Local Golf and the Kingswear & Dartmouth Golf Club by Chris Ryan 2006

Kingston Farm and its Cottages by David Williams 2008

Kingswear and Neighbourhood by Percy Russell FCA and Gladys Yorke updated by Michael Stevens and Don Collinson 2008

Kingswear Historians can be contacted at
www.kingswearhistorians.org.uk
or via www.kingswear-devon.co.uk/historians.htm

© Published by Kingswear Historians, August 2009
Printed by AC Print Ltd, Brixham

ISBN: 978-0956320018

9 780956 320018 >